To Mr Pedley, Granny & Grampy and to all those who have been affected by Coronavirus.

Mr Pedley & Grampy, you both inspired me with your storytelling, so I thought I would have a go…

Thank you to the Pigott family & my parents for all your support

THIS LAND I INHERITED

SEBASTIAN WRIGHT

Illustrated by
MOLLY MIHELL & OLIVIA TURNER

Maps produced by
JULIE WITMER CUSTOM MAP DESIGN

CONTENTS

PREFACE

I'm 18 and writing a book about parts of the world I am nowhere near fully understanding. So you're probably sat there thinking:

1. Why is this 18-year-old kid writing a book and not out with friends celebrating that school is no more?

2. Can I trust everything in this book?

Well, to answer the latter, yes you can, but understand it is my view and interpretation of the events, cultures and national perspectives. The first question is much less straightforward - I am writing this in 2020 as the Coronavirus has taken hold of the United Kingdom and of the wider world. It is a time at which nations are being tested and the impact of the Coronavirus will change many people's lives.

For me personally, my A-Levels are cancelled and quarantine is fully underway so I feel as though the best thing to do is to write a book. Why this topic? Well, I have always loved history and have long been fascinated by the way the world works. I believe the only lens to really understand today and what the future may bring is to look at how the past links to the present. I am going to write about ethnic groups and nations that often are brushed aside as they don't make the front headlines; yet I find they are incredibly insightful in understanding the way the world works outside of our immediate orbit.

My passion for history was really ignited by a history teacher during my first year of Secondary School. His name was Mr. Pedley and he completely captured my imagination. He brought history to life. My Grandfather (Grampy) has also fuelled my passion for history. So this book is inspired by Mr Pedley and Grampy and reflects my own desire to understand these fascinating nations and people. It is not a long list of my views on the current nations and their political situations, nor a political commentary. Rather, it is a historical analysis of the nations, although (as I am sure you've already grasped) not written in the most academic form.

I've long been a class clown who hasn't always paid attention in lessons, acting up for cheap laughs. Luckily I had a few people who did laugh at my poor jokes - Harry, George, Mark and Jo shared my passion for history and my joy of messing around. Hopefully this jokey tone will be clear. I do not mean to be disrespectful to any group, but nor do I want to be too formal.

School for me personally has been a struggle, a war even, with many battles won and lost. I studied History, Politics and Spanish for my A-levels and much to the surprise of probably all my teachers, I am writing a book. I have always felt constrained by the academia of school life, learning a rigid curriculum with no freedom to wander off into the niche topics that build interest in a subject. But the worst bit of the past two years has been writing essays. In class I can engage and develop answers, yet on paper I feel rushed and restricted by the strict rubric that examiners go by. This book will hopefully be a way of me finally being able to express my views in written form. Don't get me wrong, I have loved my A-levels as subject matter, the only real speed-bump has been the essay writing. So if, as you read this book you're thinking what on earth is he on about; please know that I don't blame you and now you know how my teachers and examiners must have felt.

INTRODUCTION

"Those who fail to learn from history are doomed to repeat it" - George Santayana

This book - what's it really about? Well, long story short, it is the history of certain ethnic groups and nations, specifically: the Afrikaners, the Maoris and the French-Canadians. I have chosen these particular groups because their history is an uneasy one to say the least, with them having to find a way in the midst of some very challenging odds and real oppression. Each have had an interesting history, with monumental highs and terrible lows. The borders of our political world show big straight lines drawn by colonial powers carving up the world. Thus we can see some bizarre lines that don't reflect the real cultural, religious and language boundaries. These arbitrary lines are not natural in nature and have caused ethnic groups to be lumped together and torn apart. From these imposed borders, the world has seen and continues to see the consequences - conflict via interstate and civil wars, genocides, racial segregation and many more. The fact that the borders are not right has created incredible demonstrations of unity and a coming together of cultures, and has created the worst of human nature, letting prejudice and division become engrained into societies, nations and cultures.

Just to be clear, I don't think there are any definitive reasons for why cultural groups are the way they are. Everything I write about why people behave as they do is my own theory, based on reading about what caused past events and looking at how they in turn, influenced subsequent events. Furthermore, I think it is easy to get carried away and assume that all people from a certain cultural group behave in a certain way. Generalisations are almost always bad. There I have just made one. We risk looking at groups as homogenous units rather than the collection of individuals that they really are, with personal challenges and hopes. I am confident that you as a reader will not take my writing as a definitive science. Where I generalise, it is to help understand the culture and the history. So, although we must be wary when drawing conclusions, we should still draw conclusions.

History has dealt these different ethnic groups a tough hand and what is truly extraordinary is how they have survived despite the odds. It is a real demonstration of the resilience of these people and their communities. I have chosen these three because they have had very different pasts yet all have survived. Many cultures and peoples were lost during colonisation and through social Darwinism, whereas these three have managed to thrive in their nations. They all share a British Colonial past but they exhibited different responses to the challenges put upon them by the British. It is a good way to compare the three, how they reacted to British aggression. The British Empire spread far and wide and completely altered the history of these people. Moving into the twentieth century, the three cultures showed very different attitudes, bringing out the best and the worst in human nature.

It is hard to see past the headlines and political rhetoric whether it be populist slander or liberal sensitivity. By understanding the past and the attitudes of the people that came before, we can better understand the attitudes and views of the present. I am no expert in any of these subjects, just keen to learn about the issues, and to understand the depth of these societal divides. Where some are so entrenched that they may never heal, others have already healed and the problems of the past have been left in the past.

This book is also a storybook, explaining the colourful and fascinating history of these people. The stories of how they got to where they are today are riveting. I try my best to inform and engage you but probably most importantly, involve you with the individuals. The past isn't some academic thing, rather it is the stories of those that have gone before us. This book is far from academic but I hope I inform you objectively. I have tried to research the history to the best of my ability, but when judging my historical analysis, be gentle. Each story is unique, and I tell it in its own unique way, focusing on different aspects that had different impacts. So don't be surprised if each chapter has a slightly different feel.

We all live in this world, and for someone like me who is 18 and starting out in the wider world, I want to understand what kind of world I have inherited. I know that the politics of South Africa, New Zealand and Canada have a pretty small impact on my life, however, by learning about their past, I have learnt more about mine, as so much of our history is shared. Perhaps John Donne said it as well as anyone in his poem from 1624 where he said "No-man is an island, entire of itself, every man is a piece of the continent, a part of the main.... Any man's death diminishes me, because I am involved with mankind"

I hope this book helps you engage with mankind.

PART I

THE AFRIKANERS

SOUTH AFRICA | SUID-AFRIKA

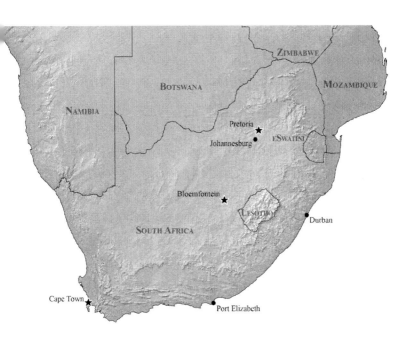

The Beginning

South Africa is often called 'The Rainbow Nation', to reflect it's beautiful diverse racial, religious and cultural make-up, embodied by the ending of apartheid. It is a land that has seen such hardship and division yet also glimmers of unity and optimism. South Africa has not had an easy past, and despite the nickname, it has not always been so harmonious - indeed, it still remains divided today. Modern South Africa is made up of several cultural and ethnic groups ranging from the Afrikaners to the Xhosa to the Zulus to many more. The Afrikaners are the most recent arrivals - white Africans, originally of Dutch descent, and make up just over 5.2% of the population. However over 13% of South Africans speak Afrikaans so the country is full of cultural and social complexities. But in order to really understand the complexities of South Africa and the Afrikaner people today, we must look to the past...

Our story starts before the Europeans arrived, with the Khoi people. Now, these folks were the indigenous population, having been there long before any Europeans rocked up, since around the year zero AD. They divided into two types: the Khoikhoi who were herders and farmers; and the Khoisan who were hunter-gatherers. They were joined approximately a hundred years later by the Bantu who would split into various groups such as the Zulus and the Xhosa. These different groups would then join together and break apart over the following centuries – so they were pretty loose terms.

Anyways, a thousand years later, in the year 1488 to be precise, the Portuguese swing by as they're on their way to India. Going around southern Africa was the only way to reach the East at this point in time. The Portuguese landed in what is modern-day Natal (which means Christmas in Portuguese). However this Portuguese trading post remained small, and it wasn't until the year 1652 that South Africa started to become properly settled. Initially, this settlement was by the Dutch and was funded by the Dutch East India Company who wanted the small settlement to act as a refreshment stop for ships going between Europe and the East Indies. The Dutch East India Company was a huge corporation that would take part in trade, colonisation and exploration. At this point in time, companies and private ventures played a considerable role in colonisation and discovery. The new refreshment stop (which is what we know today as Cape Town) relied on the Khoi for food. However, the local Khoi people were not agriculturally advanced enough for the Dutchies to depend on them for food, so in 1657 there was a large-scale settlement by the Dutch in South Africa around the Cape. Dutch farmers came to South Africa to uphold and sustain this stop-off point. These farmers would become the Boers which - funnily enough - means farmer in Dutch. The relationship between these farmers and the Dutch East India Company was hardly a happy one. The farmers disliked the taxes being put on them and wanted to expand into the interior of the Cape. Yet the Dutch East India Company did not want this refreshment stop to grow. They feared it becoming something more significant and ceasing to be just a place for sailors to take a break.

This relationship of discontent, coupled with a mutual understanding of their interdependency, continued until problems up in Europe would change the future of these little Dutch farmers. In sum, the French invaded the Netherlands in 1795, and the British wanted to keep the Cape away from the pesky French. So they decided to invade the Cape and to hold it until the Dutchies were free of the French. True to their word, in 1803 they gave it back. However, the Netherlands then allied with France, and thus the British retook the Cape in 1806. It would not switch colonial hands again.

However, this left the farmers in a very awkward situation as they were a Dutch group of people being ruled by the British, whose rule was far more invasive than that of the Dutch East India Company. Firstly, they abolished slavery, which made the Dutch farmers really dislike the British, and hence to start to want their own right to self-determination. However, it was not until the British changed the official language of the Cape from Dutch to English that the farmers realised they would have to leave. They decided to press into the interior of Africa to look for the freedom to rule themselves. And so, these Dutch farmers went on a long, arduous journey through the tough African terrain. This would lay the foundations for building a resilient people. The Dutch farmers became known as the Voortrekkers. They headed off on the Great Trek in 1835.

The Great Trek and the foundation of the Boer Republics 1835-1854

The indigenous people of southern Africa were growing and developing too. Around the year 1818 many of the native people had been united under Shaka Zulu. The spread of the Zulu empire would leave many displaced - either fleeing or being taken over by the Zulus. In this process, known as the Great Displacement, it is thought that 5 million people died. Much of the land once inhabited by native Africans was deserted as the Zulu chased them out or killed them. However, certain tribes were able to escape the clutches of the Zulus, such as the Sotho tribe (hence the reason that Lesotho exists as an independent nation today).

The Great Displacement benefited the Boers who were headed into the interior, where many of these tribes had lived. Voortrekker scouts found that much of the land was now deserted. The Great Trek was a long and testing journey through a mighty landscape. The hot African sun beating down in the height of day as these men, women and children went in search of freedom. The conditions set by the British were that the Voortrekkers had to settle beyond the Vaal River. This arduous journey into the interior took place from 1835-1840.

The group that undertook this trek was not made solely by descendants of Dutch settlers, but also those of French and German immigrants who had arrived around 1688. This mixture of groups, tied together by a common dislike of the British, would come together to form what is today the Afrikaners; their language would evolve - what was Dutch would become Afrikaans. Even before the British had got their hands on the Cape, the Boers had previously attempted to form an independent republic to get away from the Dutch East India Company. The decision - to leave all they knew behind and to take what they could in wagons into the unknown to start a new life - proved to be the start of a journey that would mould the Afrikaners into a strong and resilient people.

A depiction of the Great Trek, painted by J.R. Skelton

The journey would be a demanding test. Despite most people's perceptions of Africa as being scolding hot, down in southern Africa there are mountains where snowfall is common. The physical geography wasn't their only issue, there were hostile tribes who viewed the whites as invaders and were keen to keep them out. The tension between these farmers and the local tribes was nothing new. For years the Xhosa had been raiding their farms. The Zulus also had proved a problem, having gained the reputation for slaughtering women and children, along with their conquest of eastern South Africa which had been ruthless. However, this land was now hugely under-populated, so it was perfect for the Voortrekkers to migrate into.

These Dutch farmers were led by Piet Retief. They headed north-west into the unknown, with the desolate Kalahari stretching hundreds of miles to the west and, in the East, above the Limpopo River, malaria and disease ran rampant. Hardly an inviting place. They took wagons, carrying all they could. For months on end they journeyed into the uncharted interior until, finally, they were free of the clutches of the British Empire. But now they were in Zulu territory.

In 1838 they made contact with the Zulus. The Zulu leader, Dingane Zulu, was inviting at first, offering them land on the condition that the Voortrekkers would return some of the cattle that had been 'stolen'. When Piet Retief went to sign the treaty, he and all those who went with him, were slaughtered by the Zulu. The Zulu then went hunting and found other groups of Voortrekkers at Bloukrans. They attacked in what became known as the Weenen massacre, sparing no one. Unforgiving and relentless. They struck down men, women and children alike. In response, the Voortrekkers sent out an armed group of horsemen to fight the Zulus yet to no avail, the Zulus defeated them at what would become the battle of Italeni. The Zulus did not have guns, but they had large numbers and as those horseman rode into battle, to avenge the fallen, they used their scale to great effect. The Zulus were proving to the Voortrekkers that the British weren't the only ones with an army in southern Africa.

Depiction of the Weenen Massacre, painted by Thomas Baines

Following this, other Voortrekkers nearby were eager to

make the Zulu pay for the suffering they'd caused. These bold Voortrekkers pushed further into Zulu territory across the Buffalo river. Bravery does not even begin to describe it. Deep into Zulu territory, a scout informed them of a large Zulu army headed their way. The Voortrekkers formed a defensive ring of their wagons, known as a Laager. 20,000 Zulu warriors descended upon the Laager. The Voortrekkers outnumbered 40:1 stood bravely, determined to honour those who had been slaughtered. For hours the Voortrekkers held them at bay, - Wave after wave of Zulu soldiers charged and they were shot down by the Voortrekker cannons and rifles. The river ran red with the blood of the Zulu warriors, earning the battle the name of 'the battle of blood river'. As the Zulu realised that the Voortrekkers would not break, they retreated. The Voortrekkers then took to horseback and chased them, killing them as they fled. Around 3,000 Zulu were killed, with not one Voortrekker dead.

This event is firmly ingrained into Afrikaner folklore today as they remember those who died before them - a few hundred Voortrekkers coming together as one people to defeat a 20,000 man enemy without a single Voortrekker dying would become symbolic of the hardnosed fight of the Afrikan people. This would have another effect on the Voortrekkers - they started to view this victory as a miracle, proof that South Africa was to be a promised land given to them by God. This Calvinist way of thinking would become entrenched into the Afrikaners. Indeed, this 1839 battle is still prominent in the culture of South Africa today with the Laager having been rebuilt where it stood on the battle-field in memory of the event. It is not just remembered by the Afrikaners, there is also a monument for the Zulus who died, and it too symbolises a sense of Zulu nationalism. Following this battle, the Zulu Kingdom fell into civil war. It would be decades until they were again a power to be reckoned with.

The Voortrekkers went on to found an independent republic called the Natalia Republic, named after the British port of Natal which we know today as Durban. They were finally free from British influence. The Dutch identity was still apparent - with their new flag donning the Dutch colours of Red, White and Blue. However, the Boers' independence would be short-lived. The British began to plan their conquest and control over all of southern Africa and moved into Natal in 1842. The Boers fought the British, but this did not stop the British in their annexation of the state, turning it into the British colony of Natal in 1843.

So, it seemed the Boers' Great Trek for freedom and independence had been in vain, as the British once again ruled over them. However, as we have seen so far, the Boers aren't a people who give up, and are not a people who ignore what those who came before them sacrificed. So, in 1852, they packed their bags and once more went into the unknown. This journey, like the first, was not a comfortable one. They crossed a region known as the Drakensberg, which in Afrikaans means the 'dragon mountains', having to disassemble their wagons piece by piece and carry them over the mountains and then reassemble them on the other side. However the trek was a success, and by 1854 it resulted in the formation of the two Boer Republics of Transvaal and the Orange Free State, named after the Orange and Vaal rivers.

The Boers isolated freedom did not last. Diamonds and gold were found in the new Republics in 1867. Following this, the British reignited their interest in the region, and planned to create a South African federation, similar to that of Canada, bringing the entirety of South Africa under their control. This was driven by the British hunger for the newfound treasures. From this aspiration, the British would begin their campaign to control the entire region, with the Zulus first on the list, and soon to be followed by the Boers.

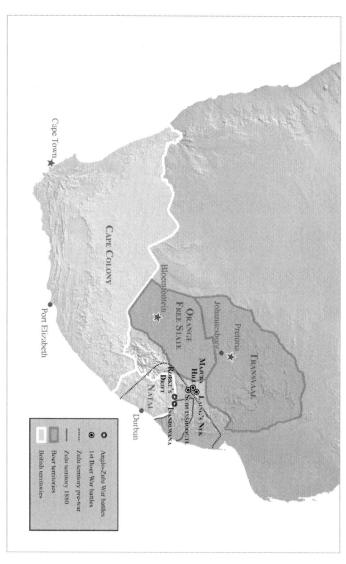

Cape Town

Port Elizabeth

CAPE COLONY

Bloemfontein

ORANGE
FREE STATE

Johannesburg

Pretoria

TRANSVAAL

MAJUBA
HILL

LANG'S NEK

ROBKE'S
DRIFT

SPITZSTROOGTE

ISANDLWANA

NATAL

Durban

Anglo-Zulu War battles
1st Boer War battles
Zulu territory 1880
Zulu territory pre-war
Boer territories
British territories

South Africa during the Anglo-Zulu War and the First Boer War

The Anglo-Zulu War

At this time the British had also set their sights on the Zulus. A people born and raised on the Savannah. Tall, strong and fearless. Only carrying humble cow skin shields and long sharp spears, they were dominant nonetheless. Decorated in beads, feathers and leathers, they embodied the terrain in which they lived, blending into the African hills, mountains and plains. They knew every nook and cranny better than the snakes that lived within them; where the water ran dry and where it flowed freely; where the fruit grew in plenty and where the roots lay thirsty. They knew which fruit killed and which fruit nourished. The lion didn't rule the savannah, the Zulu did. Trained to be warriors from infancy, they are the most famous African tribe to ever exist. My old history teacher, Mr Pedley, used to tell me stories of Zulu children being forced to wear thorns on their feet. This would toughen their feet so that they could run for miles on the tough South African floor.

Anyways, the British went to the Zulus and gave them an ultimatum they could not accept, which included demanding the disbanding of their army. The British wanted the land, they wanted all of South Africa, and the Zulus were just another thing in their way. So the Anglo-Zulu war kicks off in 1879, in which the British hugely underestimated their opponents. The British leader, General Chelmsford, feared that the Zulus would not come to fight him, so he decided to attack. This, however, was to prove costly, and this arrogance would turn what he thought to be an easy win into a long and hard-fought defeat. The Zulus were not like other native forces. They were born fighters, and unlike other tribes, the Zulus did not use guerrilla warfare tactics. Chelmsford was aristocratic, schooled at Eton College, he was bred to join the British ruling class. With short brown hair and quite the beard he was tasked to lead the British military expansion in South Africa. Having just defeated the Xhosa, the Zulu were the next to be dealt with.

When the British pushed into Zulu territory, the enemy was not to be found. Hidden somewhere in the uncharted wilderness. The South African savanna was empty, deserted, quiet. Without an enemy in sight, it looked as though Chelmsford had been right. So Chelmsford in his arrogance, ordered the three columns to part ways and meet at the Zulu capital. The main column headed for Isandlwana, where they set up camp, planning to besiege the capital. At this point, you or I would probably set up defences, call it a night and wait for the big day ahead. But Chelmsford being Chelmsford, thought otherwise. He divided his main column into two, personally leading the larger column in search of the Zulus. This left a measly 1,700 men at Isandlwana. As Chelmsford was chasing the wind, the real Zulu army was sneaking around the main column. Later, the camp began to hear reports of a vast Zulu army headed for them. Following this news, the camp commander sent a message informing Chelmsford, who was still chasing an imaginary Zulu army. Chelmsford was having none of it and wrote it off as only a small Zulu force, not the main army. He was confident they were just getting scared.

Later that day, British scouts located a small group of Zulus and chased them into a valley not too far away. As I am sure you can imagine, they weren't too pleased to find 20,000 Zulu warriors sat in complete silence, waiting for battle. Once seen, the Zulu army erupted. The scouts needed to decide what to do, and agreed that one of them leave to warn the camp, and the other few should try to fight the Zulu, while trying to escape. The scout made it to the camp, bursting in to tell the camp commander. He then sent another desperate message to Chelmsford begging for help, but Chelmsford (being Chelmsford) thought otherwise. Not long after, the Zulu arrived at the camp - 20,000 Zulu against a 1,700 British camp, which hadn't even been fortified. Chelmsford felt that fortifying the camp would have been a waste of time, despite it being standard procedure.

The Zulu had been somewhat rushed, as they had been planning to attack the day after. However, due to their innovative war tactics known as the Bullhorn formation, invented by Shaka Zulu, every Zulu soldier knew his role. The British camp commander was hardly even a soldier. His only real defence strategy was to put his men in a straight line as the Zulu charged.

A sea of Zulu warriors raced towards them. This fragile line stared into the eyes of the oncoming enemy, firing as fast as they could. The Zulu soldiers grew larger as they sprinted towards the British, charging into the swarm of bullets. The Zulu broke the British line. Overwhelmed and without support the British fought on, despite being vastly outnumbered, putting up a gritty and tenacious defence. The British soldiers refused to be beaten and continued to fight in small divided groups, often with just bayonets at the end of their rifles. They fought heroically until most were killed in a battle that those British were never meant to fight. The Zulu had not been stopped. Indeed, the battle of Isandlwana was one of the biggest upsets in colonial history - the Zulu had beaten the British.

"The last stand at Isandlwana," by Charles Edwin Fripp

A few lucky Brits escaped the slaughter and headed for a small hospital encampment called Rorke's Drift. This camp was made up of the injured and the sick, with just 140 men and various survivors from the battle of Isandlwana. Many of the soldiers weren't even part of the regular infantry. Instead, they were part of the engineering corps. So you get the picture, it wasn't exactly a well-oiled fighting machine. When the Rorke's Drift camp heard about the colossal defeat at Isandlwana, the instinct of many was to flee. However, one man kept them there, a certain James Dalton. He told the group that they could not outrun a Zulu army whilst caring for the sick and wounded. Thus their only option was to stay and fight. His inspiring talk swayed the group. Victory seemed hopeless, staying seemed foolish, yet they decided they would fight. Although hugely unprepared for this encounter with the Zulu in regards to fighting ability, the men fortified Rorke's Drift to the best extent they could. Flour bags and biscuit tins made walls. Holes were punched through the wooden walls for rifles to fire through. Beds became barricades, and finally, every soldier who could walk was ready for the fight.

I remember being taught about this war by my old teacher, Mr Pedley. I was 13 and completely entranced as he recounted the unfolding of the battle. We watched the film "Zulu" in class, and since Mr Pedley had taught in that same classroom for 36 years, it was an old small box tv, right in the corner of the classroom. The sound quality wasn't amazing, and the picture was worse, but every single student was glued to the screen. Mr Pedley would pause it every now and then to explain something, and when he did, everyone would listen. I remember his classroom for being so messy – but every bit of mess told a story. He had the remnants from an exploded grenade on his desk, he still used a chalkboard, the only teacher in the school to do so. He turned history from dull academia to real life story-telling.

Anyways, back on topic. The Zulu army was rapidly headed to Rorke's Drift, but it was not the same army that had torn the British apart at Isandlwana. Instead, it was the Zulu reserves or 'loins' who had not been used in the first battle. This force was 4,000 men. They arrived at Rorke's Drift just as the defences were being finished. They attacked at once. For 10 hours the battle roared, with every blade of grass being fought over, and the defence of each room in the Rorke's Drift building a battle in itself. The hospital was reduced to ashes and so the action moved to the cattle pens. After the long bloody day, the fight came to a close around 2 am. Only 17 British troops lay dead, although many more were wounded. In stark contrast, 350 Zulu were dead, with 500 more wounded. This had been a herculean effort, in an underdog role that the British were not used to having to fight.

Despite the almighty efforts of the men at Rorke's Drift, the invasion of Zululand had been a major failure, and the British withdrew. Chelmsford, who was left embarrassed, rushed to prepare a second invasion, and the British hierarchy who were also embarrassed, sent vast numbers of military resources to support Chelmsford. They resolved to prevent any more embarrassment. The Zulu leader at this time was a man called Cetshwayo. He attempted to bring the British to the negotiating table as he knew the Zulu would not survive the second invasion, yet Chelmsford was having none of it. He attacked the Zulu capital with cannons and gatling guns, and the charging Zulu army was mowed down. With the destruction of their capital and the defeat of their army, the Zulu Empire was no more. In this conflict, the British also defeated the Pedi, who were another tribal group, but these conflicts gained little attention – as they had neither the unwelcome defeats nor the individual bravery of the Zulu campaign.

"The Defence of Rorke's Drift", painted by Alphonse de Neuville

However, the Zulu people were not done. These stories were absorbed into their shared history, of a people comprised of strong warriors who fought until the last man. Weirdly a Winston Churchill quote springs to mind, "Nations that went down fighting rose again, but those who surrendered tamely were finished." The Zulu represent a core feature of what it truly means to be South African – having a fighting spirit, adopting a mindset that doesn't know when it's beat, and that doesn't give up. And I know that this has little to do with the Afrikaners, but I felt it a story I had to tell.

The First Boer War
1880-1881

In the geo-political picture, Britain was trying to take South Africa. So in this period, if you were in South Africa and were not British, the chances were you already had been annexed or soon would be. So at the same time as the Anglo-Zulu War, the British annexed the Transvaal, one of the Boer Republics. The annexation happened because the Government within the Transvaal had been extremely unpopular. It also faced bankruptcy from military campaigns against various native tribes. The Boers faced another problem in addition to their problems with the British. This problem was the Zulu (they hadn't been defeated by the British yet). In 1877 the British seized the moment and moved troops into the Transvaal. At the time the Boers weren't fussed about the British coming in because the situation with the Zulu was becoming dire. However, this changed after the Anglo-Zulu war and the Zulu threat had been eliminated. Thus the Boers no longer needed any sort of British protection.

Following the Anglo-Zulu war, the Boers began to take up arms, led by Paul Kruger. Kruger had lived through the Great Trek, being 10 years old when it began. Growing up in that hardship had created a headstrong and stubborn leader. He was a busy man, running a country, whilst also having 17 children. However do not let his 'active' lifestyle fool you, he was an incredibly resilient character who believed in Afrikaner independence and would fight to protect it. I think his feelings towards the British were made clear as he said "Born under the English flag, I do not wish to die under it"

Paul Kruger as an old man with a grey beard wearing a black top hat as well as pirate style earrings, taken in 1900

War broke out, much to the surprise of the British who had not expected a rebellion. The British foolishly wrote off the Boers and thought it would be an easy victory, like other wars they had fought in South Africa. However, the Boers had guns. Hence they could match the British technologically on the battlefield. It now became the job of Sir George Colley to lead the British response to the Boer uprising. By the beginning of 1881, he had an army with which he could respond. From the get-go, the British met a well-armed entrenched Boer force at Laing's Neck. The Boers were accurate shooters and snipers, and killed many British, aiming at the distinctive red coated officers. These Boers had grown up on this land, they were fighting for independence and freedom, so they fought with huge passion compared to the British who weren't fighting with nearly the same conviction. Thus Colley had to pull his men back. From there, the Boers changed their tactics. Rather than fighting conventionally, as the British were used to doing, the Boers used guerrilla tactics in which they raided communication and supply lines. The two forces then met at the Battle of Schuinshoogte, where the bright red British uniforms again made easy targets for the Boer marksmen.

So the British once again found themselves on the losing side. A month after Colley had amassed his army, Parliament in London had made it clear that they were not going to support this new war. The hangover from the costly, unpopular and recent Anglo-Zulu war was still fresh in British minds. Also, ideas of a grand South African Federation were also starting to dwindle. The British Parliament demanded that hostilities be halted and that terms of peace and British withdrawal from the Transvaal be discussed. However, Colley wasn't going to give up after a month. So he did what all mavericks do, he ignored authority. He rallied what troops he had left and marched to Majuba Hill, where the British were overrun, outmanoeuvred and outflanked by the Boers. Colley's independent thinking had only made things worse. The battle is one of the most remembered as, along with the Boer victory, it saw the death of Colley. This further defeat rubbed salt into the open British wounds in Africa, reminding many of the losses Chelmsford had faced against the Zulu. The Transvaal managed to negotiate themselves a very nice treaty - having won the war they could dominate the negotiations – with the Pretoria convention reinstating Transvaal independence.

This Boer victory stayed as a material victory - unlike the Zulu victory where, following their defeat, the British came back stronger and turned the tables. For the British, this war seemed too costly and so accepting defeat, although a bitter pill to swallow, was the sensible decision. However, the Boer Republics would not stay in isolation for long. The discovery of gold and diamonds in these lands generated massive foreign interest. At this point in time, the colonial map was being finalised, and the Boer Republics weren't going to escape the influence of the great powers. Foreign nations began to look on the region more specifically and immigrants flowed in along with this interest. The first war, which lasted from 1880-1881, was only to hint at a far larger second war which would become the largest in South African history.

The Meantime... 1881-1899

Following the First Boer War, the international situation began to take a turn for the worse for the British. They felt increasingly threatened in South Africa since Germany had taken German South-West Africa (modern day Namibia) in the scramble for Africa. British worries did not stop there as the Boers were expanding into modern-day Botswana, and the Bamangwato people had asked for British protection. Thus Britain moved troops into the area and effectively took control, expanding in the 1890s, into what is modern-day Zimbabwe. So the scales had balanced out - Britain had expanded northwards, controlling modern-day Botswana and Zimbabwe and almost completely surrounding the Boer Republics. But, the Boer Republics were not in the worst shape since the discovery of gold had made them very wealthy. The economy of both Boer Republics boomed under Paul Kruger, adding to the British sense of feeling threatened. These events conspired to start what is known today as the Second Boer War.

The Second Boer War
1899-1902

So, the British were being challenged for dominance in southern Africa by the enormous economic success of the Boers. That's where John Cecil Rhodes comes into the picture. He was an expansionist and he viewed the answer to this challenge to be to annex the Boer Republics. Rhodes mustered up a rebellion by the Uitlanders. The Uitlanders were a group within the Boer Republics who had immigrated there to profit from the gold rush, They were not Afrikaners. Paul Kruger, however, ensured that they had limited rights and were not equal to the Boers. Rhodes encouraged this group to rebel against the Transvaal. So in 1895 the Uitlanders performed the Jameson Raid, pushing into Boer territory and kicking up a fuss. The raid failed and did not have the support of London, and consequently, Rhodes found himself out of a job. This now gave the Boers a genuine reason to prepare for invasion. Since the British had shown signs of aggression in the Jameson Raid, almost all in the Republic recognised the threat of British invasion. Now Kruger could justify buying arms and preparing men for combat. They began to arm themselves, and due to the success of their economy, they could buy plenty.

Following this, the German Kaiser sent Kruger a message congratulating the Boers on their victory. This, obviously, made the British fear that a German-Boer alliance was forming. Another British concern was that the Boers continued to spread across southern Africa with a few getting all the way up to Angola. As a response, the British began to amass an army along the borders of the Boer Republic. In 1899, Paul Kruger (President of the Transvaal) and Marthinus Steyn (President of the Orange Free State) sent an ultimatum to the British demanding they withdraw from their border. The Boers were not going to be bullied into submission. The British refused, and the war began in October 1899. For the first three months of the war up to 1900, the Boers dominated the British. They defeated the British at the Battles of Colenso and Magersfontein and successfully besieged both Mafeking and Kimberly. Home trained and determined, they proved quite the fighting force. With slouch hats and beaten down clothes they took on the professional British army.

Boer guerillas during the Second Boer War

The Boers were fighting on their land. As Ray Heron said, they knew "the heights of the hills and the widths of the valleys, the depths of the rivers." They also had other benefits which the British did not, such as immunity to many African diseases. The Boers were being attacked by the British and thus did not need to take the fight to them. And the impeccable Boer marksmen were able to pick off many Brits.

It was clear that the British had underestimated the Boers yet again. Like they did with the Zulus, they came back stronger with reinforcements. So in January 1900, many thousands of British soldiers burst onto the scene, changing the dynamic of the war. The war had been in the balance, and despite a British defeat at the Battle of Spion Kop, they recovered both the cities of Ladysmith and Kimberly by February. Soon after the capital of the Orange Free State, Bloemfontein, would fall to the British. By May, Mafeking had been retaken, and in June both Pretoria and Johannesburg had been conquered. However, despite the conquest of the Boers' land, the British had not ended the war.

Boer Soldiers in a trench at Mafeking, 1899

The Boers would not be defeated that easily, and resorted to guerrilla warfare tactics. This was a state-ment of resilience like no other - the British could take all the land they liked, but they'd have to crush Boer spirits to win the war. The Boers again caught the British off guard, and the 250,000 British troops failed to keep the region under their thumb. The British realised that since they could no longer hit them on the battle-field, they would now hit them in their homes. The British began scorched earth tactics - burning the homes, land and farms of the Boers. While the men were out in the country, the women and children were sent to concentration camps. It is thought that 28,000 died with 22,000 of those being children. However, due to their resilient nature, and despite this horror, the Boers continued to fight. Ultimately, the Boers would fall, however, and peace was made in 1902. The two Boer Republics now ceased to exist. Boer nationalism, however, still roared on, and as they moved into the 20th century, they would find themselves in positions of power. The century that was to come would see one of humanities darkest moments, Apartheid.

The Union of South Africa
1902-1914

The British "big picture" plan was to create a federation in South Africa. In this new Union, the Boers would find themselves in a position of power as Blacks lost the limited power that they had. South Africa was to enter a period where race would become the dominant issue, and Blacks were not viewed as equals to Whites. Throughout the entire century that was to come, the relationship between Whites and Blacks would be clear - Whites in control, Blacks facing institutionalised racism equating to discrimination, violence, and exclusion. The relationship that would be less clear would be that between the white British and the white Afrikaners. The Blacks outnumbered the Whites about 5:1. It was clear that the English whites and Afrikaner whites would have to work together to ensure control over South Africa. In many ways, the Boers had lost their Republics and gained all of South Africa.

But I am getting ahead of myself. After the end of the Second Boer War, the British plan to make a federation of South Africa started to come into fruition. By 1905 all four of the separate colonies had agreed that it would be beneficial economically, and the railway system was expanded, along with the removal of many customs. In the various conventions building up to the Union of South Africa, no Blacks would be invited to have any say in the foundation of the nation. And so, in 1910, when the Union of South Africa happened, two Afrikaners were placed in charge. Louis Botha would be the first President and Jan Smuts, the first Prime Minister (kind of like a deputy). Both had been generals in the Second Boer War for the Boers. Although it seemed that this could cause problems, in practice both realised the importance of reconciliation between the British and the Afrikaners if they were going to survive.

In contrast to this unity at the top, there was a growing sense of Afrikaner nationalism, and in 1914 the Afrikaner National Party came into being along with several other Black political groups. The African People's Organisation (APO), founded in 1903, became a voice against the all-white government, and in 1912 the South African Native National Congress was founded. Despite these groups, the Whites began to introduce institutional separation, i.e. the laying down of the Apartheid which was to come. In 1913, the Land Act was passed, giving Blacks less than 8% of the land. Worse, Blacks could not own, lease or purchase property outside of these zones. This was the beginning of the state of South Africa. This balance of power, enacted via the Government, ensured that Blacks would remain subjugated and powerless. The Afrikaners and British, in contrast, had secured control over the region.

World War I

World War I broke out in 1914, and with South Africa under British control, they were dragged into the war. However, South Africa, as we know, is not as simple as Whites and Blacks. The Whites were themselves divided. The majority of the English were supportive while, in contrast, the Afrikaners were less so. The Boer concentration camps and the defeat in the Second Boer War were still in recent memory so, for many, fighting for Britain felt wrong. The initial involvement for South Africa was to attack (successfully) German West Africa and then German East Africa. The majority of the troops were English South Africans, with few Afrikaners in comparison. Following the invasion of German West Africa, some Afrikaners rebelled, as many Afrikaners lived in the region. This rebellion was put down by Botha and Smuts, yet, being Afrikaners themselves, it seemed as though they were putting down their own kind. This fuelled Afrikaner nationalism. So, while the German West Africa campaign was a military success, it is important to understand that it was a success for the British rather than for South Africa. For many Afrikaners, this was not their war.

The inequalities faced by Blacks continued through wartime as they could not be soldiers. Rather, they took on other roles - such as the Labour Corps, which aided Smuts in his German East Africa campaign. Some Black South Africans went to Europe to fulfil general tasks such as dealing with supplies. Many South Africans would die in the war – overall more than 146,000 Whites; 83,000 Blacks and 2,500 Mixed Race and Asian South Africans served in the war. The story of Black South Africans in World War I is a largely untold one. Their main role was building infrastructure and clearing battlefields after the main fighting to pick up the dead bodies. It was a duty that saw many Blacks die as they were still perceived as targets by the enemy. When these soldiers came home from war, they were not decorated. So I wanted to acknowledge their sacrifice and show them the respect they deserve. Meanwhile, the Afrikaners were more worried about getting out of the war.

Many Afrikaners fought, despite their concerns. It is often thought that World War I was only fought in Europe. However, the fight over German, British and French colonies was very real. Prior to the war, Germany had four colonies in Africa, of which one was German South-West Africa. So it was inevitable that the border between British South Africa and German South-West Africa would become another front in the war. From the get go the South Africans had a majority in numbers. Botha and Smuts had one eye on the battlefields of German South-West Africa and another eye on the Afrikaner response. Afrikaners lived in German

South West Africa too. Anyways it is safe to say that the Germans were conquered quickly despite putting up some resistance in the beginning. By July 1915 the South African troops had their feet up enjoying the sun. The main point is that German South-West Africa was no longer German.

South African forces using a 4.7 inch QF Naval gun in the desert

South African officers pose with a captured German flag in Windhoek

Where the battle of Africa got really interesting was in German East Africa. Following the victory in South West Africa, Smuts was put in charge of leading the South African efforts to take German East Africa. This is modern day Tanzania, Burundi and Rwanda. It is far from South Africa but the conflict felt very close to home. It saw South Africans fight the Germans but more perhaps more interestingly some Boers went to fight for Germany. So now it seemed Smuts was quite literally fighting his own people.

Smuts would not steamroll the Germans like he had in South West Africa. The fighting here was tough. The main reason was that one of the greatest generals of the 20th century was leading the Germans - Paul von Lettow-Vorbeck. His tactical cunning and dominance on the battlefield earned him the nickname of "The Lion of Africa". At the beginning of the war, a treaty had allowed German colonies to stay out of the war. However, Vorbeck was keen to get them involved. He knew that causing trouble in Africa would distract British efforts, taking focus away from the Western Front. He intentionally provoked the British by destroying British infrastructure in British Uganda.

From the start, South Africa was on the back foot. Vorbeck had beaten Britain's larger and better armed forces on several occasions. However, things changed when Smuts took South-West Africa and hence the South Africans were able to join the fight. In addition to the extra troops, their arrival boosted the morale of the

British troops that were already there. It's safe to say that Britain did not want to have to fight this war. Smuts job was to quickly end it, so the troops could go to the Western Front in Europe. Vorbeck knew he could not match the military strength of Smuts and the Empire. They outnumbered him and had better equipment - Smuts had 250,000 soldiers to command, while Vorbeck had just 22,000.

Vorbeck had some early victories but did not become arrogant. He knew that he did not need to "win" the war, a draw was a victory in that it kept the South African troops there so that they never went to the Western Front. To make things worse for him, Portugal joined the war against German East Africa so they were fighting another army as well.

The future of German East Africa looked bleak. All resupplies had been blocked and no troops were coming to support them. Vorbeck took up guerrilla warfare tactics. The South Africans would now suffer from the very tactics the Boers had used themselves in their fights for independence. Vorbeck could not afford to lose men so these tactics made sense. He moved his forces to the south of the colony, where there were hills and tall grasses, giving cover for ambushes. Smuts could do little.

Vorbeck also utilised local tribes. Although technologically primitive, extra resistance gave the British another problem. Vorbeck used more than 12,000 natives even though, prior to the war, they had been bullied and killed by the Germans. Vorbeck forced them to fight. Unsurprisingly, the war was terrible for the local people, as armies on both sides took their food and destroyed the land so their enemies could not use it.

Gradually Smuts managed to push Vorbeck's men back. The German troops were forced into Portuguese East Africa, where they looted and seized the food and resupplies they needed. Smuts was becoming increasingly weary that Vorbeck had no intention of fighting a war head to head, in a conventional style of warfare. This war was costly for Smuts in terms of the actual war and the fact that some Boers were fighting for the Germans. Many Afrikaners thought Smuts had sold them out to the British, and overall there was little consensus among the Afrikaners themselves about how they felt about the British. Smuts was something of an exception, in that he had positive views of the British. But overall the way that he was perceived as being so friendly with Britain heightened Afrikaner nationalism.

Smuts needed to defeat the Germans but Vorbeck's objective was to prolong the war, keeping the South African troops in East Africa and in that he succeeded – this campaign turned into the longest campaign of the entire war. Even following the armistice in 1918, the war in German East Africa raged on. Vorbeck understood that direct conflict with the enemy would lead to defeat, but picking them off when resupplying or travelling would continue the conflict. Vorbeck did eventually surrender following orders direct from Germany. In many ways you have to say Vorbeck won this war as he achieved his goal – ie. to keep South African and British troops away from the Western Front.

Notwithstanding Vorbeck's efforts, South Africa (like most British Empire colonies) was pulled into active fighting in Europe. One defining encounter for those South African men was the battle of Delville Wood, which was part of the larger Battle of the Somme. The South Africans role was clear – remove all German soldiers from the wood. The soldiers, being both Afrikaners and English South Africans knew it was a tough ask but stormed the wood. Much to their surprise, they succeeded but soon came to realise that this was the easy part, and that keeping the wood would be the real challenge. The orders from British high command were clear: defend the wood 'at all costs'. It was clear, retreat was not an option.

The South Africans took a beating. German artillery tore them apart. The constant bombardment came at 400 shells a minute. If that wasn't enough they had to fend off the advancing German troops as well. I am genuinely staggered by how these South Africans held firm. Isolated and alone, in the face of an enemy who threw the kitchen sink at them, somehow they held on for 6 days of pure hell. If the Boer wars hadn't been hard enough on the Afrikaners this surely was. After 6 days backup finally arrived to find the forest was gone. Trees that had grown up over decades were now mere stumps. Mud made the terrain nearly impenetrable. When people talk about 'no-mans land' this is exactly what they are talking about. Completely lifeless. 100s of metres with nothing living. On one side, the British Empire and its forces along with the French; on the other the Germans. There were only 750 South Africans left. They had listened to that order telling them 'at all costs' word for word. More than three quarters of the South Africans died. As a nation, they had not seen such destruction in such a short amount of time and, for the Afrikaners, it seemed that Britain had again brought them conflict and death.

An abandoned German Trench in Delville Wood

World War I showed the Afrikaners unwillingness to

fight for Britain. However it also brought an incredible awakening within the White population. A sense of identity, recognising the sacrifices and role in both Africa and the Western Front, developed. Those who opposed the war, who were the majority of Afrikaners, now gained political traction.

After the war, some industries such as mining became destabilised. There was an increase in production costs coupled with lower demand so generating difficult economic conditions. Many mine owners wanted to use Black labour. This obviously was not welcomed by Whites who viewed their jobs to be under threat. Three-quarters of the White workforce were Afrikaners, yet the industrial leadership were mostly English South Africans. South Africa saw many strikes through 1907-1922 with rising discontent. For example, the South African Communist Party was founded in 1921. During the 1922 strikes, things escalated out of control. Smuts had supported the mine owners and ordered that strikers should be dispersed. At one factory in Benoni the strikers were bombed and 153 people were killed.

In this period racial legislation continued to pass through the government, further institutionalising segregation and racism. For example, the 1923 Land Act created residential segregation in the urban areas - Blacks could no longer live in the city, they could only travel into the city to work. In 1924 the National Party and the English Labourites joined together to form a pact. Thus, Smuts was pushed out and made leader of the opposition. The pact was weird - the National Party were strong Afrikaners who were nationalists, in complete contrast with the English Labourites. This is when the National Party, led by a man called Hertzog, began to pass laws to benefit Afrikaners and the Whites generally. One example was what would become known as Hertzog's 'Civilised Labour Policies'. These policies basically ensured that unemployed Afrikaners replaced Black workers and got paid more (specifically on jobs relating to the rail network.) There was the creation of laws which protected Afrikaners' jobs. Not only did he create an economic division between Whites and Blacks, but he would also further the already divided social elements of society. He promoted Afrikaans as a language and removed Dutch as an official language.

At school our house matron was South African, White but not an Afrikaner. She tried to teach me a bit of the language but, since I am not a natural linguist, it felt like gibberish. It is very similar to Dutch as it descended from it. Mr Pedley's approach was that to speak Dutch all you have to do is stuff some sugar cubes in your mouth and try to speak normally. Dutch and Afrikaans are similar and even though Afrikaans has evolved over the years, it is still very similar. 95% of the language is of Dutch origin. The native southern Africans have adopted the language as well - for example the word for Marijuana is 'Dagga' and gogga (meaning insect) both come from the Khoisan language. Matron's husband, Paul, was an Afrikaner, and left a very positive impression on me. Anyways, I am getting off topic.

In 1929, white women gained the vote, yet this, despite being beneficial for women, was damaging to the Blacks as it pushed them further into political minority – i.e. the few Blacks who could vote became increasingly less influential as there were now even more White voters. During this period, South Africa became more independent from Britain, along with many other countries in the Empire.

The South African economy was impacted by the Great Depression, and many white farmers suffered. In 1936 Hertzog and his parliament passed the Natives Trust and Land Act and the Natives Representation Act. This removed the vote from any Black. The divide between Whites and Blacks was widening, and the economic hardship fell disproportionately on Black communities. Despite Hertzog and Smuts being old rivals, in 1934 they had formed a coalition. Although both were Afrikaners and already very supportive of a White-dominated South Africa, they were not extreme enough for many Afrikaners. So in 1935, DF Malan and others formed the 'Purified National Party'. This would be the party that would take power in 1948 and create apartheid in its full form.

Through the economic hardship Afrikaners had been growing in influence in South African society. They were increasingly involved in policy formation and the media, with English Whites less so. Afrikaner nationalism was becoming a serious movement harking back to the days of the Great Trek and the Battle of Blood River with actual reenactments. The defeat in the Second Boer War was still heavily embedded into the minds of Afrikaners. As they grew in power, they were very protective of this status - one explanation for the apartheid that was to follow. They were simply scared of losing control again, and the Black population was the largest threat to them. There were various funds to help Afrikaners grow economically, and Afrikaners were incentivised to hire Afrikaners rather than English speaking Whites. Many Afrikaners also held strong Christian beliefs. Since the Great Trek, they had believed South Africa to be their promised land, and they were the Chosen People. Afrikaner Nationalism would ultimately push many of the English speakers out of South Africa. Afrikaners were becoming increasingly exclusive in the way they ran institutions and society.

<u>*World War II*</u>

South Africa involvement in World War II was a divisive issue for many South Africans. Even though they entered the war, many people were opposed. This opposition acted as a catalyst for a more radical Afrikaner movement and hence World War II further helped the Afrikaners grow in power. The South African role was substantial, with them being pivotal in the East Africa Campaign. Blacks still didn't really take soldier positions, but were often on the front lines and heavily involved in building projects. The war also proved instrumental in the growth of women's role in South Africa, for example, the foundation of the Women's Voluntary Air Force. Despite South Africa serving wholeheartedly in the war with many volunteering and their impact in Africa being considerable, there was another side to it...

There was a growth in radical Afrikaner groups, some even wanting a Nazi victory. A group called the Ossewabrandwag, or OB for short, wanted a German victory and a similar Nationalist-Socialist style government in South Africa. Prior to the war, they were just a social group. Yet, after the war they became a paramilitary group and attempted to sabotage Smuts and his government, modelling themselves on the SS in

Germany. They were pro Germany and viewed the Afrikaners as a chosen people. At this point in time, Afrikaner nationalism was taking a darker path, and other radical groups were popping up, like the 'Nationalist Socialist Rebels'. These groups never gained widespread support like the Nazis in Germany, but they crept into South African politics, and as the future would show, ideas that had been extreme were no longer out of the question. Indeed, two of South Africa's future leaders were members of the OB.

There is one story that I came across when speaking to my mum. She knows an amazing amount of obscure and sometimes random information, but this one was a real gem. She told me of women pilots in World War II and their role of flying planes from the factories to the RAF bases, without radar or guns. They often flew through dogfights without any sort of defence on board. Now, why am I telling you this? Well, having done some digging, I came across an Afrikaner woman called Rosamund Everard-Steenkamp. She is a true heroine, although often forgotten. Born in the Transvaal in 1907, she was a tough and resilient character who was eager to fight in the World War. She looked for opportunity wherever she could, joining the Russian air force as they recruited women for combat. Following this, she made her way to England where she ferried aircraft fresh out of the factory to the RAF bases. Her only navigation aid was a small handbook. No radar or anything. Somehow she did it, overcoming all the limitations put on women in this period.

Rosamund Everard-Steenkamp

Potentially the most famous Afrikaner in the war was Adolf Gysbert Malan. Obviously, Adolf wasn't too popular of a name given the circumstances so he became known as Sailor Malan. He was one of the war's greatest fighter pilots. He was quick to join the British Royal Air Force, rather than the South African Air Force. He wanted to be in the thick of it, having signed up in 1937. In Dunkirk he became an Ace, which is an accreditation won after shooting down 5 enemy planes. He fought tenaciously in the dogfights among the fleeing soldiers. Overall, he gained 27 victories in the skies, a monumental number and was the RAF's top ace at the beginning of the war. He was overtaken as his flying days were cut short, being retired from active operations in 1941. In Britain's darkest hour, when it looked as though the Nazi war machine could not be stopped, an Afrikaner was the Allies' greatest pilot. Later on in his life he also opposed Apartheid and became very vocal about the racist regime, calling for its removal.

Sailor Malan climbing into a Supermarine Spitfire

When thinking of the allied air force in World War II, several stories from my Grandfather spring to mind. He grew up near a US Air Force airfield in Northampton-shire. It was an exciting time to be a 10-year-old boy, watching the planes take off, and when returning, sometimes seeing trailing black smoke, often with their engines blown out. He distinctly remembers the 'Black Thursday', where 18 American planes took off to bomb German armaments factories. They were gone all day - Grampy described their return: "Darkness was approaching at Chelveston when the ground crews heard the sound of engines and could not believe that only two aircraft had returned."

Anyways, back to the Afrikaners. As noted, South Africa's role in the war was significant, especially within Africa. Their air force played a significant role in slowing Mussolini's advances. Mussolini, the Italian dictator, had a vision for Italy to reclaim the territories of the Roman Empire so he aggressively pushed into northern Africa. The South African air force was crucial in winning the air war and thus the whole region.

One aspect of the South African World War II story is often forgotten, namely their invasion of Madagascar. Following France's quick capitulation, the Nazis created a puppet state called Vichy France, which was effectively just Nazi Germany but under the French tricolour. Therefore Madagascar, as a French colony, was an enemy state that was way too close for comfort for South Africa.

Invading Madagascar was always going to be difficult since it would require an amphibious attack to land on the island. Madagascar may have felt distant and irrelevant to winning the wider war in Europe, but its location made it an important naval base. Positioned between Europe and the Asian colonies, was capable of seizing anything passing through its shipping lanes. So, for the British war effort, of which South Africa was part, it was important to take the island. This worry was fed by the continuous aggression from Japan. The Allies were concerned that Madagascar could be used as a base for Japanese submarines. Japan could thus compromise all supplies going to the European colonies in the far east, which were needed for the various invasions. This vague concern was made very real when Vichy France said they would cede Madagascar to Japan. Now, Churchill and Smuts knew they had to act. Operation Ironclad came into being. Churchill and Smuts were very close and, as Smuts paid more attention to the Empire, he paid less to Afrikaners back home, raising a feeling of abandonment and hence heightening Afrikaner nationalism.

The war effort for the Allies was already a massive logistical headache with supplies needed to prepare for the Battle of Britain. Planning a totally new seaborn attack added to the problems. It is 450 miles between South Africa and Madagascar, and to make things worse, Madagascar had a defence force of 8,000 men. Although not a large number, they were fighting on land they knew very well. They also had small air and naval forces. So there were very real risks of failure. The joint British and South African leadership planned to make Port of Diego Suarez the focus of the invasion. They felt that if they took the port, the rest of the island would fall relatively easily. The invasion was led by the British but the actual fighters were South Africans with a few Australians, supported by the British and Australian navies.

So on 5th May 1942, 15,000 men, with a group of special forces and 6 tanks invaded (while much of the island is mountainous, the coastal plains are flatter, perfect for tanks). They landed on four beaches on the tip of the west side of the island. The South Africans encountered little opposition at first, although one tank got stuck in the mud. They pushed across the 20 miles to Port of Diego Suarez, where the fight really began. The South Africans had caught the Frenchies off guard but the defenders held firm. The South Africans decided to attack the Port front on by using their tanks to lead the offensive. However, the terrain was open and the French artillery made quick work of them. So the South Africans launched a flank attack but they got bogged down in the swamp to one side of the Port. To make matters worse, the South African radios broke so they could not communicate.

The fight had become a stalemate until a British ship changed the course of the battle. HMS Anthony went head on into the port, crashing through the defences and enabling 5,000 Allied marines to surge ashore. They wreaked havoc in the port area as now the defenders had to watch their backs as well as their fronts. The Allied forces were too strong and the Frenchies surrendered just 2 days after the invasion had begun. However, the rest of the island stood firm, much to the annoyance of the Allies, who now had to push through the island, the very thing they had hoped they would not have to do. The mountainous terrain in the centre of the island was challenging, and helpful to the locals, fighting on home soil. Then, on 29th May, the Japanese joined the battle, confirming the suspicions of Churchill and Smuts. Four Japanese submarines started to pick off Allied ships. A midget submarine snuck into the port, sinking an oil tanker and damaging a Royal Navy ship. Also, while the Australian navy had been helping attack Madagascar, they had left Australia open to attack. Five Japanese midget submarines made their way into Sydney harbour, killing 21 sailors and shaking civilian morale.

The invasion of Madagascar dragged on and the Allied leadership decided to relocate many of the attacking force as successes became fewer and less frequent. Much of the South African Air Force was sent to Europe and much of the various navies present went to help the US in the Pacific. Many British troops were sent to India. It seemed the invasion was falling apart at the seams. However, South Africa stayed and indeed, added soldiers. They slogged on, looking for Governor Annet, the leader of the Vichy defenders. He remained hidden in the green rolling hills of the centre of the island. It was very tough since there were relatively few soldiers on both sides compared to the large island of Madagascar. Encounters became rarer, and became almost a game of chance encounters between the Allies and Axis soldiers.

Long story short, it took three more naval invasions on various parts of the island to subdue Madagascar and to get the Vichy French to surrender the colony. As the battle had gone on, so did the South African role in leading it, showing that South Africa was gaining an unofficial autonomy within the Empire. This part of WWII is often overlooked but was an important aspect of the wider global conflict helping the Allies keep the European and Pacific theatres connected. Although isolated, these Vichy French soldiers fought tenaciously, indeed, these 8,000 men resisted the invasion longer than France had resisted the German invasion. It was a gritty and ferocious war.

There are few records kept over whether the South African soldiers were Afrikaners or English. However what is clear is that, as Smuts grew fond of Britain and the Empire, and did their bidding on the world stage he forgot his own people. He indirectly caused the growth of Afrikaner nationalism as many Afrikaners felt he had become institutionalised by the British Empire.

Post War and Pre Apartheid

Following the war, there was a change. DF Malan was leading the Purified National Party (NP) which had become a loud voice for Afrikaner nationalism, heralding back to the old Boer Republics. They sang to those who the war had not benefited. They mainly gained support from those whose jobs had been lost and those who were scared of a future where Blacks could compete with the already struggling Whites. The economically difficult times created a class of Afrikaners who viewed the only thing stopping them from falling into poverty was keeping the Blacks below them. Smuts had been going with the times - internationally, across the world, racial laws were beginning to relax, and Smuts had allowed Blacks to live in urban areas. However, many scared Afrikaners disagreed, and DF Malan promised a policy of Apartheid in response to this fear, promising to protect Afrikaners. It was becoming clear that the 1948 elections would be a choice between apartheid or no apartheid. Hertzog left Smuts and joined Malan, and Smuts lost the election. He had been favourite to win, and many never thought that the NP could win Smuts died two years after this.

I personally view Smuts to be a genuinely great statesman who was able to remove past prejudice to build a new South Africa. He convinced South Africa to go into WW2, thus helping to defeat the Nazis, and he became one of the main forms of opposition to apartheid. Although he had put laws in place that caused great difficulty for the Blacks, towards the end, following WW2, he began to look as though he was following a line of desegregation. Furthermore, I am a firm believer that we should judge a person by the standards of their own time, and by those standards, I hold Smuts in high regard.

I've got a mate from South Africa called Tanaka. He's black, and I asked him what he thinks when he hears the name Smuts. He said that he thinks of the famous Jan Smuts Avenue in Johannesburg. He told me that people are divided over him. He was essentially one of the founding fathers of the country, and he proposed the idea of segregation. Yet, his views did change, and ultimately he opposed apartheid, and supported policies of reconciliation. So although not perfect, he did amend his ways and fought valiantly against fascism.

In 1948, a new era would start, an era from which South Africa still hasn't recovered. The NP won the 1948 elections and put in place apartheid. They reformed the military to ensure Afrikaner dominance and Afrikaner nationalism became institutionalised.

Apartheid

Apartheid was the segregation of Whites and Blacks. It was one of the most extreme forms of institutionalised racism the world has witnessed in the modern era. What is quite so shocking about Apartheid is that it lasted until 1994. To put that in perspective, the Simpsons had been running 6 years before Blacks gained any sort of rights in South Africa. Apartheid was fully established following the 1948 election which the NP won and enabled the complete oppression of Blacks and any Non-Whites in South Africa. This would prove to be South Africa's darkest hour.

From 1948 onwards, new laws and acts completely divided the nation based on race. The new policy caused every member of South African society to be classified into a racial group, and from this all their opportunities, rights, and economic strength were be decided (the Population Registration Act). There were four groups: Black, White, Coloured and Asian. Apartheid was reinforced by laws which only permitted certain races to live in certain areas - Blacks could no longer live in White neighbourhoods. Land belonging to Blacks was taken by the government and given to the Whites (the Group Areas Act). The government's stance was that the Blacks had their land, and the Whites had theirs. However, obviously, it was not that simple, and the Blacks were not free even in their land. They were still governed (and suppressed) by the South African government, which was all White. Apartheid further engrained racial segregation into the social aspects of society - the Prohibition of Mixed Marriages Immorality Act barred Blacks and Whites marrying. Segregation did not stop there, segregation would go down to the smallest levels of society, now parks, restaurants, public transport would all be segregated. The Blacks were being dehumanized as the government systematically removed their rights.

While at school, I had a tutor in my house who had spent a portion of her childhood in Zimbabwe. Now I know that Zimbabwe has had its fair share of problems racially, but South Africa had racism everywhere. She told me about how whenever she and her family would go into South Africa, she felt uneasy. I remember her saying there was tension in the air that Zimbabwe didn't have. She recalled one time she and her family took the train in South Africa. As they got on, an Indian man was escorted out of the carriage despite there being plenty of free seats. He was moved into a packed carriage full of other non-Whites. He had to leave the carriage because White people had come on. She said that it was a level of racial awareness she had not experienced before, and she became very conscious of her race when in South Africa. It is hard to imagine, leaving Kings Cross in London on a train to Yorkshire and suddenly, people being forced out the carriage because of their race.

Apartheid was active during the Cold War. It was perhaps an overly simplified world where it was "East vs West" and in South Africa, "Black vs White". Since South Africa was a western country, communists were viewed as a threat to society. The government removed opposition via The Suppression of Communism Act. Those who spoke out against Apartheid were labelled as communists, and Nelson Mandela would actually be arrested under this act. So you get the picture... there was relentless political action taken against the Blacks. Their land was taken, they were removed as citizens, and they were separated from Whites in all forms of life. Everything from where you could sit on trains to where you worked was decided by race.

So how did such a repugnant system get so entrenched? How could those who had been removed from the political system create political change? Well, international circumstances were beginning to change. Throughout the 20th century, colonies of empires turned into independent nations. Empires that had lasted for centuries, covering every inch of the globe now started to shrink. The world was entering a new phase and, as the world changed, so too did Africa. A giant had been woken and many oppressed people gained their freedom. The best example is India and the movement that Gandhi led. Many African countries were beginning to establish their independence, e.g.

Ghana in 1957. The formation of opposition did come to South Africa despite no real political opportunity to do so. It came through the ANC (the African National Congress). This first opposition took hold via the Defiance campaign in 1952. The campaign saw boycotts and civil disobedience. The ANC thinking was that if the Whites wouldn't listen to reason, maybe they would listen to their wallets. This is where Nelson Mandela first got involved with the ANC. However, this campaign failed to bring any meaningful change so the Pan African Congress was formed, which was far more aggressive. The group took the view that peaceful protest had got nowhere, so now violent action was the only way forward.

Naturally, tensions increased, and this tension ultimately snapped in 1960 in Sharpeville where the police opened fire on a crowd of unarmed Black protestors. Peaceful protestors mowed down as they stood, demonstrating for their freedom. Women, men and children alike – lives ended by machine guns. That day saw 69 killed and 180 wounded. Sharpeville proved to be the catalyst that saw violence become a central part of the anti-apartheid movement. Violence begat violence in return. Let's not forget that Blacks were being beaten and killed by White policemen already. This was nothing new, as the local population had experienced years of brutality and oppression from first the Dutch, then the British, and now the Afrikaners. The police would beat and kill Black men and cover it up. The system protected them. Indeed, this was Apartheid's purpose – a system designed to keep the Black man down and the White man in power.

After Sharpeville, the government clamped down and outlawed the ANC, labelling it a terrorist organisation. The violence continued, and the ANC continued with their hardline violent response. Mandela was arrested and was tried for treason, for which the punishment is death. However, Mandela avoided the death penalty, and instead was sentenced to serve life imprisonment. He actually served 27 years before he was released. While in jail, Mandela became the figurehead for the anti-Apartheid movement, and he became a global icon. I recommend watching the film or reading the book 'A long walk to freedom' to get an understanding of both South Africa during this period and of the man himself. The anti-Apartheid movement grew in strength, and in 1976 there was an uprising in Soweto. The students protested that the Afrikaans language was forced on them and how in school they did not receive a proper education but rather learnt to wash dishes. In response, the government mowed down the young student protestors. This stirred up more support for the anti-Apartheid movement. In the struggle against racial oppression, many lost their lives aspiring that their descendants would have equality, justice and democracy. We should never forget just how much was given so that future generations can be free.

Apartheid by this point was seen as globally disgraceful, and the whole world put pressure on South Africa to change. Sport can say a lot about a country and South Africa was banned from the Olympics because of Apartheid, yet the real backbone of South African sports was (and still is) the Springboks, the national rugby team. They were an all-White team for so long, and as Blacks have become more and more involved in that side, it demonstrates to me personally a nation that is evolving. During Apartheid, many Blacks supported whoever was playing against the Springboks. The fact that today, the entire nation rallies behind the team, which in 2020 is led by a Black man, demonstrates a real coming together of a nation.

Now that you understand the Black movement and how it evolved, we can focus on the Afrikaners at this time. So… in 1958 Hendrik Verwoerd came to power. For the African continent this was a period of independence and the formation of nations. Remember that South Africa was the culmination of several different people groups. All these different groups had very different cultures and histories. So Verwoerd thought he would divide the nation so there would be land for Blacks (called homelands) and land for Whites. However, this could not work to any sort of benefit for Blacks as South Africa was so intertwined. By moving Blacks to different sections, it only made them poorer and removed from any sort of economic opportunities. It was utterly unrealistic to think he could descramble

South Africa to create independent states of all the different peoples.

Anyways he was assassinated in 1966 and the fella who took over from him, John Foster, continued with this misguided idea for the following decade. After these two had had their go at socially engineering South African society into what it could not be, a man called P.W.Botha came to power. He saw the problems and realised that reform was the only way forward, not some over-elaborate theory of 'separate development'. Botha changed Apartheid, removing many of the most sinister laws. For example, Whites and Blacks could now marry; Blacks could now move with greater freedom around the country; and Coloureds and Indians were moved into the same racial class as Whites.

This progressive change only encouraged the Black movement, giving hope and Blacks began to believe in their own emancipation. However, removing the Indians and Coloureds from institutional racism had little effect on the Whites effective hold on power. Whereas freeing the Blacks would cause the Whites to lose all political power. If a "one man one vote" system were put in place, the Whites would lose their ability to rule, as the blacks greatly outnumbered them. The Whites held other fears - they worried that they'd also fall into chaos if they gave Blacks the right to vote. Much of Africa had proved an example of how not to create a peaceful transition. They also feared the communist presence within the ANC. Due to the aggression of the USSR in southern Africa (Angola & Mozambique were communist), many feared any sort of communist influence in the country.

Although Botha made massive reform, he did not remove Apartheid. As much as he tweaked it, ultimately, it would have to be removed. In 1989, F.W. de Klerk took over as the South African leader. Short and bald, an unlikely hero. He wore wiry type glasses, the real 1990s look. From the get-go, he made it clear that huge change needed to be made and that South Africa needed to be transformed. De Klerk was a strong Christian and viewed it as his purpose from God to emancipate the Blacks and to take South Africa into a new era. De Klerk released all the ANC prisoners apart from Mandela, he allowed Blacks to protest, and there was greater political expression in general. As is well known, he and Mandela negotiated the ending of Apartheid, perhaps surprising many people in the process. Personally, he had nothing to gain and everything to lose, yet he did it because it was the right thing to do. What amazes me is that there was not a violent outcome, the talks were peaceful and remained that way, much to the credit of both Mandela and de Klerk.

de Klerk (left) and Mandela (right) shaking hands at The World Economic Forum (Davos) in 1992

The problem of the Soviet influence had gone away. The war in Angola in 1987-88 saw the Soviets lose interest in the region, and 50,000 Cuban communist troops in Angola were removed. Following this, Namibia was able to gain independence, having been under South African rule since World War I. Economically, the Blacks had become stronger, and Whites were less dominant in the economy. However, let's not get ahead of ourselves, Whites were still in very much in control, but at least, Blacks were becoming more involved in all aspects of the economy.

It is clear that Apartheid is a stain on both South African and the world's conscience. While originally it was similar to the rest of Africa and indeed to the southern United States, what is so shocking is that it lasted for so long. By focusing on the Afrikaners, it is clear that they had imposed one of the most horrible political systems the world has ever seen. Apartheid is pure racism - driven by power-hungry people, but also by a scared people. A people who had experienced so many attacks on their own freedom. They finally had gained control and did not want to see it lost to people they viewed as below them. The Afrikaners constructed a system that would lift up Whites and push down Blacks. The Afrikaners could not allow their right to self-determination to be questioned, they wanted sovereignty over their people. The Afrikaners handled this horribly. However looking at the bigger picture, these problems arose because, in many ways, South Africa was never meant to be a state. It has different people groups with different cultures and whose histories are mainly united solely through many wars against one another.

Life after Apartheid

The ending of Apartheid led South Africa into a new era, one of hope and equality. Due to the one man one vote system today in South Africa, Blacks broadly control the political system. So these Afrikaners who have fought for 200 years to rule themselves are now again an awkward situation. And I am sure that some of you reading this think that it is what they deserve. My view is no it is not. For South Africa to heal as a nation all peoples must be brought together, rather than divided further. I am not saying that past wrongs should not be addressed, but South Africa must look to the future, not the past.

South Africa today is a economically strong nation in contrast to other African nations. However the price was great as colonial genocide against native peoples and generations of exploitation and oppression were endured so that colonists and Afrikaners could rule. We should never forget how much was lost by native populations in the imperialistic colonisation across the world. Their story is one of suffering but also incredible strength as many have now found their liberation. Africa is moving on from its colonial past as nations across the continent continue to grow economically. I think C.S.Lewis put it best when he said "You can't go back and change the beginning, but you can start where you are and change the ending."

My dad worked in South Africa in 1996 following the end of Apartheid. He said that among white South Africans there was a sense of hope, a general feeling that the nation was really modernising and moving forward. It was still a strange society – for instance, he did not really work with any Blacks as they were still not in leadership positions in major companies. It was also a dangerous society where people routinely ignored red traffic lights at night to avoid being vulnerable to a car jacking.

However, the identity of Afrikaners has changed, as South African identity has too. Afrikaners are now more connected with other South African groups than ever, and the division between groups pales in comparison to that which existed just 30 years ago. The nation has become more integrated, although divides are still blatant. Afrikaners are now governed by non-Afrikaners and as we have learnt, for Afrikaners, the freedom to rule themselves is of utmost importance. When looking at the issues of South Africa today, we see that the separate ethnic groups have caused many of the current problems. Fundamentally, the Afrikaners are not a racist people but a people who feel threatened and want to protect themselves.

The future of Afrikaners will be like their past, an uneasy one. Their role in South Africa will continue to shrink and where they go from here will be an interesting journey to follow. Yet, if there is one thing we have learnt from their past, it is that they are an incredibly resilient people. From Dutch farmers to Voortrekkers to Boers to Afrikaners. My politics teacher told me that South Africa is a country with a very colourful and dark past, two words that aren't often used together. Yet that is the best description of South Africa and the Afrikaners - there is so much variety. We can see inspiration out of their struggle yet also moments of utter darkness and horror.

I think the right way to end this chapter is a quote from Nelson Mandela. A man who represents so much of what modern-day South Africa stands for, a man who embodies the struggle of the South African people and one who has created a better future.

"Do not judge me by my success. Judge me by how many times I fell down and got back up again." - Nelson Mandela

PART II

THE MĀORI

NEW ZEALAND | AOTEAROA

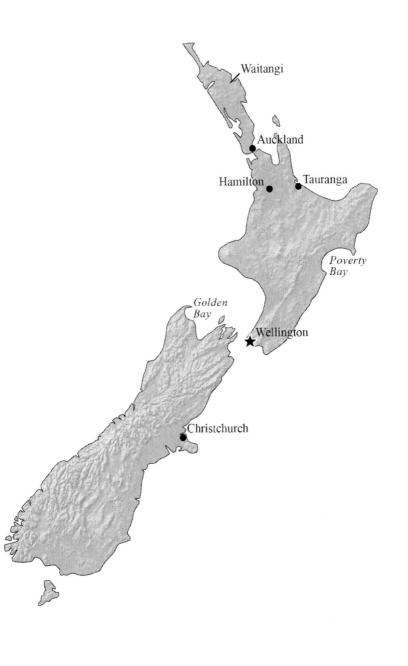

The Beginning - The first Maoris

New Zealand, a place where the hobbit was filmed and where the national animal is a small defenceless fluffy bird. A gentle place. However, there is nothing defenceless or gentle about the Maoris. They encapsulate the many conflicts and contradictions of New Zealand. They are a people whose history is steeped in warfare, being fierce and honourable warriors. New Zealand however, is a peaceful place - there are no natural predators, and it is a very habitable land. In Maori, New Zealand is called Aotearoa, which means the land of the long white cloud. It is ironic how such warrior people live in such a peaceful place.

New Zealand politically today shows this peaceful nature. The coming together and unity between indigenous and foreign peoples is like no other modern former colonial country. You only have to look at the Haka, a traditional war dance performed by the national rugby team which is made up of both whites and Maoris. It is a real tribute to the unity of the two people groups, which is so rarely found in countries that were colonised. However, the past has not been easy for the Maoris and the fact that the Haka has become so symbolic of New Zealand as a whole is a testament to them: a people accepting others into their culture in spite of a challenging history.

When Abel Tasman first discovered New Zealand, the Maoris sent a fleet to engage in battle. Unlike other natives the colonials had encountered, the Maoris took the fight to them. They are a unique culture. For instance, they are not like the Australian Aboriginals, who have lived in Australia for thousands of years. The Maoris haven't even lived in New Zealand for one thousand years. New Zealand is a young place. It is thought that the first people arrived around the 1200s. To put that in perspective, the University of Oxford has had students longer than New Zealand has had people living on it.

New Zealand was the last chunk of land to be inhabited by humans. The first Polynesians to come to New Zealand were thought to have arrived around the year 1250. Throughout this period they settled on the coast, in various different villages, mostly on the North Island where it is hotter, and the terrain is less hostile. It was not until the years 1400-1500 that the Maoris really started pushing inland. Obviously, most of this is historical guesswork as the Maoris did not keep written records. When the Maoris arrived, they brought with them new animals and challenged the existing ecosystem. For instance, they hunted the famous giant flightless Moa bird to extinction. The local food chains had evolved in complete isolation and birds filled many roles usually filled by other animals. Even today, New Zealand doesn't have any snakes, and their import is prohibited. The environment that had developed in New Zealand was so delicate, and something like snakes could cause radical change - a little Kiwi bird versus a snake will only end one way.

'Hunting Moa birds from Extinct Monsters: A popular account of some of the larger forms of ancient animal life *1892.'*

But we digress…. the ancestors of the Maoris spread across the Pacific into Polynesia from their origins in South East Asia. They got all the way to Easter island. There is even evidence to suggest that the Polynesians who started in South East Asia made it to South America - Polynesian DNA has been found in parts of the population in Chile. Over time their languages changed along with their culture and appearance. This long process of migration across the Pacific led to the first Maori finding themselves in New Zealand. The people who would settle to become the Maoris had conquered many miles of open water, using nothing but the stars, winds and currents as navigational aids. New Zealand was just one of the many islands discovered by these wayfinders. Maori legends teach that the first Maori to find New Zealand was a man called Kupe. Kupe did not settle, but rather he journeyed to find new lands for his people. He and his companions journeyed on great ships called Wakas, which could survive on the vast Pacific Ocean. Driven by curiosity and the need to expand, the Maori found New Zealand, initially the North Island, but spreading down to include South Island.

These initial explorers were clearly a well-organised people, having to settle the new lands with only what they had been able to fit on their ships. The Maoris in many senses are known as the natives, yet they have only lived in New Zealand some 600 years longer than the white immigrants who would start to arrive in the late 1700s. Despite the Maori and Europeans having very different cultures, they do share the common historical theme of coming to New Zealand in search of something new... something better.

The Maoris believed in various legends and multiple Gods, to explain how things came to be. Perhaps the most well known of these Maori Gods is Māui, made famous by the Disney film "Moana". The legend of Māui is strong evidence that the Maoris originally came from the same place as people in the rest of Polynesia. The legend of Māui can be found in one shape or another across almost all of the Polynesian islands. He was this mischievous character who would pull up islands out of the Ocean for people to explore and then settle. The belief is that Māui pulled up the North Island and that the South Island was his canoe and the Stewart Island was his anchor.

Myths and legends are engrained into the Maori culture. The idea of being connected to your surroundings by both the physical and the spiritual is a common theme. The Maori religion was one of inheritance, understanding that you have inherited this land and that all things are connected through the passing of time. Most Maoris hold that six gods rule over six different aspects of existence (although the details vary from tribe to tribe):

- Tūmatauenga, the god of war, violence and hunting

- Tāwhirimātea, god of weather
- Tāne, the god of the forests and all that lived in them
- Tangaroa, god of the ocean and all the fish
- Rongo, god of peaceful actions such as farming
- Haumia, god of the uncultivated land and the foods that naturally grow.

The Maoris view of these gods is different to how Westerners think of god. They see the gods as being the personification of the earth, giving it life and character, so people feel more connected to their environment. For example Tāwhirimātea, the weather god, has a very intriguing backstory. He was the second oldest son of 70 children, all of whom were boys. Six were other gods while his parents were the Mother of Earth and the Father of the Sky. His brothers wanted their parents gone so that they would be the most powerful gods but Tāwhirimātea disagreed. He aligned with his father to seek revenge on his brothers. Together they had many children, who became the spirits of wind and storms. So all weather in New Zealand is a child of Tāwhirimātea. A son and father having children is a weird thought, but that's the story so just go with it.

Tāwhirimātea destroyed the forests of his brother, Tāne, and then sent Tangaroa, the sea god back into the ocean. He continued on this path until all his siblings retreated to their mother. Tāwhirimātea now gathered his children to fight a huge battle - all the different types of weather, from whirlwinds to hurricanes, came together to attack and much of the land was flooded. From this were born the great lakes of New Zealand. Meanwhile, Tūmatauenga, the war god, so angry at his brothers for being beaten that he created hunting, fishing and cooking so that their lands can be subjugated by humans. Such stories are common in Maori mythology - connecting the physical land to the people, personifying the natural elements. It also shows just how war was so engrained into all aspects of their lives, even religion. All the tribes share these stories, but often with their own little twist. And if that wasn't complicated enough, there were other Maori gods, with some tribes having up to twenty gods.

Ancient Maori culture had one feature which it is still recognisable today. Tattoos. The Maoris have incredibly beautiful and complex tattoos, which are signs of heritage and identity. For example certain patterns show that you are from a specific region in New Zealand. Today, symbols can be representative of personality traits and what your life has entailed. Traditionally, they showed your tribe and your status within it. The tattoos often cover arms and the upper torso. As Maori people age, they add more tattoos to show seniority. In Maori culture the head and face is considered the most sacred body part. Maori men would have their face covered in tattoos, while women often have tattoos around their lips and chin. The tattoos were and are traditionally done via a shark's tooth or other suitable bone, sharpened and dipped in the pigment. The tattooist hits the bone or tooth into the skin with a mallet thus piercing it and leaving a tattoo. Through all this, the person being tattooed was expected to not make any noise.

So you get the picture – before the European "discovery", the Maoris had developed in isolation. Their society evolving to consist of hundreds of different tribes all with their own subcultures, but sharing a common language and culture of war.

European Discovery

Abel Tasman… Another Dutch explorer finding another part of the world. In 1642 Tasman led an expedition to Asia and became the first documented European to set eyes on New Zealand. A few people reckon that the Portuguese were the first to find it, but there is no proof, and it is widely accepted that Abel Tasman was the first to see the islands. In Europe at the time, empires were forming, and the Dutch were one of the big players. The same drive for exploration that had driven the Maoris to New Zealand was now at work in Europe, with the same outcomes.

Tasman first saw New Zealand off the coast of the South Island. Initially there were no signs of life, until smoke appeared in the sky from inland. Tasman soon found himself in New Zealand's Golden Bay, and he felt it would be perfect for European settlement. These calm waters and European like climate were perfect - a more appealing northern Europe. The area was green and covered in woodland. You and I can only imagine how chuffed Tasman was to have found this idyllic land. He must have been over the moon. However, this tranquil image was broken by the sight of Maori war canoes heading out from the shore towards them. These long Waka boats were packed to the brim with Maori soldiers. Tasman's optimism faded, as he realised these were not friendly vessels. The Maoris attacked by lobbing spears onto the Dutch boats. A few sailors were killed or injured but spears could only do so much. Tasman ordered the sailors to fire upon the Wakas and, unsurprisingly, guns beat spears. A few Maori were killed so the Maoris, confused and bewildered, retreated. Both sides were left shaken - the Maori confused by the technology of rifles and Tasman intimidated by the bold and confrontational Maori. Tasman left the bay for the safety of deeper water. Tasman had given the Maoris their first sight of a people different to them. They had no reason to believe that such people existed - it would have been like seeing aliens.

Depiction of Murderers' bay by Isaack Gilsemans, a Dutch artist who joined Tasman on his journey. This was one of the first images shown to Europeans of the Maori. Drawn in 1642.

It would be another 100 years until Europeans would

return, this time in the form of Captain Cook and his ship, The Endeavour. Cook came from the east and, having travelled through parts of Polynesia, had made contact with many of the natives of those islands. However, none would be as warlike and aggressive as the Maori. Cook found the coast of New Zealand in 1769, making landfall on what is now known as Poverty Bay. For the first three days, there was no sign of life, until smoke was seen rising inland above the green woodland. Cook, excited by his new discovery, took two small boats ashore. Leaving four men to watch the boats, the rest pushed into the uncharted wilderness. As Cook and his men were pushing inland, the men at the boat were confronted by four Maori, who gradually became more aggressive. One grabbed his spear and, as he was hurling it, was shot. The sound of gunfire carried through the thick forest. More shots followed. Cook, obviously concerned, rushed back to his men. The Maori were bewildered by the unknown tech-nology of rifles and retreated. Cook took his men back to the Endeavour.

The following day, Cook made a second attempt. He went ashore, this time with a man called Tupaia, who was a Polynesian that they had taken as a translator. Obviously, his language and the Maoris were different, but they were similar enough (as they had the same Polynesian roots). Cook was probably a bit naive to think it would all be fine having killed some Maoris the day before. Once again, violence broke out, and many

Maori died but not before they had a crack at kidnapping one of the British sailors. What they wanted with him no one knows (maybe they wanted to eat him, I will let you decide that bit). Cook again returned to the Endeavour without any real communication established. What had become clear was that the Maori weren't scared, and had no problem fronting up to rifles. Cook was curious - it was clear that the Maori were not like other Polynesians he had come across. After these contacts, Cook stopped trying to approach the Maoris, but instead, he mapped the coast.

New Zealand would stay isolated for only a few more years. Cook had confirmed the existence of a new land, perfect for European settlement. The Maoris isolated existence was about to end.

European Settlement

Cook's map of New Zealand and his changing of the name (from the Dutch Nieuw Zeeland to the English New Zealand) laid the foundations for a British claim on the region. After the loss of the 13 colonies in the American war of Independence in the west, Britain was looking more eagerly to the east. They were also looking to supplement Britain's timber industry which could not keep up with demand. So Cook explained to the "powers that be" in Britain how the tree-covered New Zealand would be perfect for a British Colony. As well as the timber, many headed to New Zealand in search of whales and seals. Indeed, it was these whaling fleets that brought the first real European settlers of New Zealand.

These settlers soon realised the aggressive nature of the Maori, but they also noticed how the Maori traded with one another. The British had a lot to gain with a native population that was willing to trade. However, the trade being conducted by the Maoris wasn't the same as European trade. Rather, it was based on goodwill and swapping things like for like, and was more about building good relations between tribes. When the Europeans began to trade with the Maoris, the Maoris quickly caught onto the competitive nature, and were also fascinated with the new inventions of Europe. However, this would not have a peaceful ending. The Maoris would start to use the latest technologies to settle old scores while the British would begin to settle in pockets across both islands. The bulk of the settlers had not yet arrived and these additions would start to change the balance of power.

The Musket Wars 1807 - 1842

So, the Maori had lived on New Zealand for ~600 years, developing trade networks, alliances and rivalries. A delicate political and social system had formed. The introduction of new technology in the form of muskets would see the destruction of much of what those 600 years had produced. Giving these weapons to a people who were so aggressive and hungry for war would prove devastating. Maori warfare had been continuous and, although it was vicious, it was small scale, mainly hand to hand combat. But that all changed when British merchants in Sydney started trading weapons with the Maori for food. The Musket Wars began with the Maori realisation that muskets could lead to military dominance.

The man to start this was Chief Hongi Hika, from the Ngāpuhi people. Based in the northern peninsula on the North Island where Maoris were densely populated, Hongi Hika decided to attack the neighbouring tribe of Ngāti Whātua. They came together at the battle of Moremonui. Now, it's all well and good having muskets... but you need to know how to use them, and it is pretty safe to say that the Ngāpuhi didn't. It took Hongi Hikas' men over 20 seconds to reload. So the

Ngati Whatua were able to make the battle hand to hand. Armed only with muskets, Hongi Hikas' men were clubbed to death. Two of his brothers died in the slaughter – their heads chopped off and taken as trophies. Once the battle was over the Ngāti Whātua ate the dead bodies of their enemies. Hongi Hika, somehow, survived this. He fled into a swamp with a few other survivors.

So Hongi Hika suffered a humiliating defeat, and he wanted revenge. However, he didn't let one bad battle deter his faith in the muskets. He saw the benefit in the guns and stuck with them. He trained his men better and, when action came again, history did not repeat itself. He won the battle and soon looked southwards. He needed to produce more food to get more firearms from the British merchants over in Australia. So he raided the south to enslave the population. These slaves produced as much food as they possibly could, and almost all of it went to the foreign merchants, resulting in bucket loads of firearms pouring into the North Island. There was so much trading of food that now the Maoris were starting to go hungry themselves.

Hongi Hika was no slouch. In 1820 having completely changed the dynamic of the region, he went to England where he was treated like royalty with gifts and whatnot. The trip's formal purpose was to create a Maori dictionary but, while he was there, he tried to get more weapons. To no avail. It is probably not surprising that

King George IV did not give him the keys to the castle and every piece of weaponry he could ever want. But the trip was not a waste of time - on the way back Hongi Hika stopped off in Sydney where he exchanged all the gifts he had received in England for 300 muskets. These new rifles would put Hongi Hika in control of the region, with no one able to challenge him. Obviously, the other chiefs were not happy with this, knowing that they were now at the mercy of a pretty ruthless man. So an arms race began, as the other chiefs scrambled to find firearms. Tribes to the north of Hongi Hika were quick to arm, securing a respectable number of muskets, so that he would have to seriously weigh the benefits of attack versus the potential casualties. Meanwhile, to the south, the tribes didn't arm themselves to nearly the same extent. So Hongi Hika attacked the south, and his invasion was composed of wave after wave of victories. The southern tribes were in a state of shock, having gone from clubs to muskets in just a few weeks; but they managed to find some weapons and soon their fightback would begin.

A sketch of Hongi Hika by a British General in 1820

This war would cause the death of up to 40,000 Maori men, women and children. The conflict spanned both islands. Their warfare was being fundamentally upended and Maori society with it. Many Maori were also dying due to European diseases to which they had no immunity. Thus, in this time of cultural chaos, many abandoned their gods and became Christian. This was partly because the British were not dying – so the Maori thought the Christian God was protecting them and that their Maori Gods had betrayed them. These people had gone from the stone age to the industrial age, coupled with worldwide trade, all in the span of a few decades.

Anyways, back to the storytelling. Hongi Hika's Ngāpuhi tribe found themselves allying with various other tribes in the north of North Island. The alliance's goal was to raid south and effectively colonise the other Maori. However, Hongi Hika would not see the end of this war as he died in 1828, perhaps fittingly killed by a musket shot. His impact on New Zealand and the Maori people is colossal, completely changing the society. Following his death, the mighty Ngāpuhi would not stand dominant for much longer and would fall from their height, ultimately fading into history.

So who was going to fill the void? A man named Te Rauparaha took centre stage. He was nicknamed the Napoleon of the South, and he was one heck of a general. He would lead his people, the Ngāti Toa, to become the dominant group in southern part of North Island. He allied himself with Hongi Hika's former people so that, as they faded away, his people took their position of dominance. However, stronger tribes had evolved in the north of North Island. They were pushing Te Rauparaha south so, as he moved south conquering the local smaller tribes, his previously conquered land would be captured by the dominant tribes of the north. This process of conquering and moving south for the Ngāti Toa people would be known as the 'The Migration'. It doesn't quite have the same gravitas or excitement as "The Great Trek" does it? Anyway, by the early 1830s, this migration was coming to a close as the tribe of Te Rauparaha came up against the southern coast of North island. The Ngāti Toa managed to secure the south but Maori inter-tribal relations were a mess at this period in history - with new wars and feuds popping up on a regular basis.

So the Musket Wars were coming to a close. During all this, the British had been slowly doing quiet land grabs over the island. As the Maoris had been fighting themselves, fuelled by British rifles, the British took control over much of the land, giving vast chunks of land to white farmers. Te Rauparaha, unlike Hongi Hika, would unify the Maori in a fight against the British. But the 30 odd years of battle had taken their toll on the Maoris, and they were now tired and fatigued, while British settlements continued to prosper, reinforced by waves of new immigrants from Europe. It was clear that some sort of agreement between the British and Maoris would have to take place – either granting Maoris some form of independence or being annexed by the British. To us now, it is clear that annexation was going to happen no matter what the Maori efforts. However to the Maori warriors of the time, they could not see that and they would not give up their land that easily.

So, the Maoris and the British would ultimately settle their differences on the battlefield in the New Zealand Wars. It is evident that the British wanted nothing less than annexation and the Maoris wanted at least to keep their land. The Maoris and the British ended up signing the treaty of Waitangi in 1840, which was one of the founding documents that would see Britain take control of New Zealand (not least to ensure that the French did not!)

The Treaty of Waitangi - 1840

During the Musket Wars, Europeans had begun to settle all over New Zealand. As permanent settlements grew, so did the inevitable desire for formal recognition. New Zealand was evolving from a revenue opportunity for those over in Sydney to a new colony in its own right. Most settlers were British and Irish coming for the timber, whaling or seal furs trade and or to spread the Christian gospel. Some came from Australia, having been sent there as criminals.

As their numbers increased, British Maori conflicts looked inevitable. You get the picture, a load of Brits rocking up while the Maori were fighting themselves, so that tension between the two groups grew and so the Maori would go from fighting one another to uniting to fight the British. As the Brits settled mainly in Auckland, they looked south and saw the warrior Maori, where the most powerful tribes resided, so they began to get nervous. This fear was actually unjustified as the Maori had their eyes set on one another, with several tribes fighting for the top spot, and feeling they needed the Europeans for trade. However, Maori fears of the Europeans were also rising – as the European numbers grew from 2,000 in 1840 to 20,000 in 1850. Most of these immigrants had come for land, which was precisely what the Maori were fighting over. The Treaty of Wait-angi is probably the most influential document in New Zealand history, as it laid the foundations of formal and legal Maori - white relations. However, it led to multiple disagreements over land claims. Much of the confusion was down to inadequate translation, with both parties having a different understanding of what the treaty meant.

However, the most significant issue related to uninhab-ited land that had been bought by the British. They felt they now owned the land and that was the end of the matter. However, a large chunk of the land had not been bought legally, and so was really still Maori land. Anyways, this disagreement created a hostile rift between whites and Maori. To the British, any land not lived on by the Maori was free game for British settlers and this was legitimised in the treaty. To the Maori, such settlements were theft of the most valuable commodity in their culture and society – land repre-sented history, religion and more. As we have just seen from the Musket Wars, territory was vital. So when the British began moving into these lands, they were met with some resistance. The British stopped the formalities.....

The New Zealand Wars
1845 - 1872

When the British began taking New Zealand by force, they encountered the most robust native population they had ever had to deal with. This was before they met the Zulus. Although the Zulus really would be the toughest native force, the Maoris fought so uniquely that they brought some unexpected challenges. For example, they wanted to fight at a pre-arranged time to obey their formal code of war. It was important to create a fair fight between warriors, with a level of honour in Maori society such that, even if they lost, the warriors had done so having faced their enemy. It was as if the British were fighting a European war, on the other side of the world. No hiding in trees and the hillsides, ambushing supply lines, but rather formal, orchestrated, clashes on the battlefield.

This strong resistance by the Maori led to a bad outcome in Australia for the Aboriginals. When the British started looking for land in Australia, the Aboriginals were treated to a far more aggressive approach from the British. Many were simply slaughtered. Murdered on the spot. There was no diplomacy nor potential trade discussions as there had been in the early days of New Zealand.

So in 1846, the first proper British-Maori conflicts broke out along the Hutt Valley. It was several Maori tribes against the British, after the Brits had expanded into Maori territory. The New Zealand Company had made a deal over the land – but conflict arose as to where the border should be. The British, thinking this was their land, brought in troops to push the Maori out. Concurrent with the skirmishing, Governor George Grey was pressuring the Maoris to sell more of their land. The British bought the South Island, cheap as chips, on the basis that it would be a reserve for the Maori. Perhaps unsurprisingly, the British ignored this aspect of the agreement and started to populate the land with white settlers.

Governor Grey was a reluctant fighter, despite his order to send in troops. He traded with Maori and often met their chiefs in good faith. In fact, he even wrote to the King to say the two people groups could live together. However, at this crucial point, the Big Cheeses in Britain ordered Grey to head off to Southern Africa, where (as we know from the last chapter) British interest was rising.

After his departure, relations between whites and Maoris deteriorated. The number of whites continued to skyrocket, and by 1860 there were 60,000 in New Zealand. The pressure on land intensified and the Maori were now outnumbered in their homeland. What could the Maori do? It was clear that the treaty of Waitangi wasn't going to protect them, and starting a war would end in tears, as they knew from the Musket Wars. So they decided to try to get the Brits to the negotiating table. They knew that if they were divided they had very little chance. So they found themselves a leader, a representative to negotiate with Britain on behalf of all of the tribes, to try to ensure that Britain would stick to the formalities of negotiation rather than pick off the individual tribes with military force. They wanted to create a system where Britain and the Maoris would talk regularly to sort out issues.

A Maori village, taken sometime between 1860 and 1889

The new King of the Maoris, Pōtatau Te Wherowhero, had a lot going for him - he got on with the Europeans and was very well regarded among the Maori. However, he was getting on, and after two years he died. His son, Matutaera Tāwhiao, took over.

Matutaera instantly hit problems. The first being a new land dispute. He was unable to keep either the Brits or the Maori happy and war broke out in New Plymouth. In reality, he probably could not have done much as I reckon Britain just wanted the land. The new British governor, a chap called Browne, poured in troops; but the tough Maori had fortified well. Hundreds died on both sides, and there was a hefty bill at the end, with substantial damage. Unsurprisingly Governor Browne was sacked. In his short tenure he had managed to turn a good-natured relationship into an aggressive one. So the Brits recalled Governor Grey from Southern Africa.

However, Grey would not be able to rekindle the relationship he once had with the Maori as Governor Browne had done enough damage to burn multiple bridges. Obviously, Grey did not start with perfect trust on either side – as there had just been a substantial conflict. He knew there would be animosity. However, Grey felt the Maoris were doing more than just defending themselves. They were challenging his rule and going against the treaty of Waitangi. So he wanted to prove who was in charge. Grey also needed land. More Europeans were arriving every day, and all wanted a slice of the pie. So he had massive pressure on him to get the Maori to sell more land for new settlers. However, it had become very apparent to the Maoris that losing land meant losing wealth, power and any sort of independence.

Grey thought if he couldn't pressure the Maori into

doing it, he might trick them into doing it. He attempted to set up Maori councils to support the British and question the Maori king. He failed. So Grey tried a different trick – he wrote to London, describing a big revolution that was brewing and suggested that the Maoris were about to seize Auckland. This was all a lie, most Maori were loyal subjects of the crown. But the deception worked and he got a load of fresh troops to help him. Grey gave the Maori an ultimatum - completely surrender to the British Empire and submit yourselves to Queen Victoria or Britain would invade and take the land by force. But Grey was getting used to being devious, and indeed became outright slimy. He attacked before the letter with the ultimatum even reached the Maori chiefs.

War soon spread across the whole North Island. The British outnumbered the Maori – with 14,000 soldiers against only 5,000 Maori of whom only 2,000 men could be in the field at any one time. Even though these 5,000 were no pushovers (they had fought in the Musket Wars) and they knew the lay of the land, they were no match for the better armed, better resourced and ulti-mately more united British. Various battles occurred, almost all in the North Island, and Britain won the majority. The result was harsh land confiscations.

There were many different conflicts that came under the title of the 'New Zealand Wars', I mean there were a lot. The British just picked them off in small conflicts, fighting each tribe individually. The main conflicts were

Wairau Affray, Northern War, Hutt Valley and Wanganui campaigns, First Taranaki War, Invasion of Waikato, Second Taranaki War, East Cape War, Titokowaru's War and Te Kooti's War. They were all caused by the Brits looking to annex Maori land in one way or another.

'The Death of Von Tempsky at Te Ngutu o Te Manu,' a portrayal of an incident in the New Zealand wars on 7 September 1868. Painted by Kennett Watkins.

During the wars, in 1854 to be precise, the first New Zealand parliament formed in Auckland. Initially, there was no Maori representation. However in 1868 the first Maoris were elected to the parliament, and thus a path for airing Maori issues had been formed. Although the multiple wars and various European diseases had been hugely damaging for the Maori, as the century progressed, it looked as though the Maori would not face the same segregated society as the blacks in South Africa or the Aboriginals in Australia. Indeed, in 1893 women got the vote. [New Zealand was the first major country to do so, although the Isle of Man had given this right to women in 1881 and various other countries gave women conditional rights]. This progressive move from the government at the time gave more hope for the Maori, as they looked for more political representation.

Land Confiscations

The war ended with the British having forcefully asserted their dominance over the region. 700 years of Maori independence and sovereignty ended as New Zealand became a fully functioning British Colony, rather than the Crown Colony created by the Treaty of Waitangi in 1840. Although the war ended, the incoming tide of white immigrants continued and land pressures increased. However, now the Maori were pushed off their land, not with military force but with legalities. This "asset stripping" continued until the year 1900.

The "New Zealand" wars had, in reality, been many different wars fought between the British and several different tribes. Small disagreements often grew into military conflict. There seemed nothing to stop more disagreements and similar conflicts from continuing. The British thought about how to break this pattern and, in 1863 passed the "New Zealand Settlements Act" to allow them to confiscate land from any Maori tribes that they viewed as opposing British rule. This Act was followed, in 1865, by the "Native Land Act" to reduce apparent confusion and to provide them formal control. These laws required that Maoris prove their ownership of land, and introduced an array of legal proceedings.

The Maori people in general didn't understand or have enough wealth to fund such legal matters. So it seemed that the British had beaten them on the battlefield and were now beating them in the courts. Hence, many Maori just sold their land rather than bother going through the bureaucracy. The new settlers continued to arrive and the Maoris continued to be pushed off their land. Frankly, the Maori struggled to adapt. Several land confiscations were politically motivated or simple acts of revenge to punish the Maori for the war in general or specific uprisings. The Native Land Court institutionalised removal of Maori from their land, requiring all Maoris with titles to come to the court to submit their title for review. The British court would often fail to recognise their title and thus take the land. Through this process the Maori tribes broken apart, and individual Maoris began to join the British society - to the extent they could – by taking manual labour jobs. Land purchases went on relentlessly.

By the year 1900, Maori land ownership was reduced to small slithers of land, disconnected from each other. The Maoris were now fully marginalised. In this year, Maori politicians proposed the "Maori Land Administration Act" in an attempt to protect the remaining Maori land. It was to no avail – the ongoing land ownership transfers continued and New Zealand society (as we would recognise it) was starting to develop. The Maori's future would be determined by their reaction to the past century of hardship and subjugation.

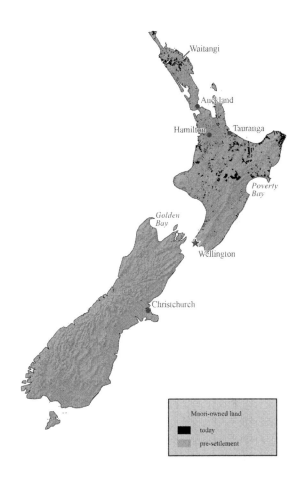

Maori-owned land today versus prior to European settlement

A New Century

So, we arrive at the start of the new century with the Maori in a mess – their population had suffered immeasurably; their land had been confiscated (legally or by force) and their political rights were limited. Yet something changed as they went into the 20th Century. The Maori population started to increase and there was something of a political awakening as many decided to try to legally reclaim land that had been unjustly stolen from them. Maori MP's grew in numbers, and hence so did their influence. Maori councils began to gain power and carry out policy, bringing the first early signs of potential coexistence.

Let's not get carried away - while Maori councils ruled over some parts of the land, whites now owned much of the property. Although there were different schemes to ensure that Maoris were able to grow economically, it was still at the margins. And the tide turned again so that by 1910 many of the councils had dissolved. There seemed no burning desire from the Maori for them to exist as Maori society changed with the times. They fused into the white culture and moved away from hereditary tribal roles. They moved towards a merito-cratic system where people earned their roles based on ability and they began to embrace the competitive nature of our "western" society.

In 1909 the Young Māori party was formed. It was basically comprised of a bunch of well educated Maori boys who had studied at a western school. They were not like most Maoris of the time, who were illiterate, and they caused further divisions within Maori society. The party, in many ways, was advocating for the Maori people to move into western society, on the basis that the alternative was to be destroyed entirely. This was perhaps the springboard from which, through the coming century, Maori lives and rights would change drastically.

A war started on the other side of the world. When Britain declared war on Germany in 1914, New Zealanders had little interest in a far away conflict – especially with their own history of wars over the last 60 years. But New Zealand had no real choice in the matter, they were owned by Britain, and were expected to help. In fact, thousands of men signed up, thinking it was the next big adventure, and New Zealand committed wholeheartedly to the conflict to the extent that nearly half the able fighting population ended up fighting. New Zealand and Australia came together to form the Australian and New Zealand Army Corps, or ANZAC for short.

To kick start "their" war, New Zealand took Samoa. It had been under German rule, but the Kiwis weren't going to allow any enemy territory in their back garden. This was the first seizure of German territory in the entire war. The main conflict was far, far away from the shores of New Zealand, and for many men, it was their first time away from New Zealand. Many soldiers went to Egypt to train. Overall 18,500 Kiwi soldiers died in World War 1 and they fought all over the globe; from the hot, dry unforgiving Middle East to the cold, damp relentless Western Front. But it was the heroics of the

ANZACs at Gallipoli that are probably most inspirational and most well known. From 1915-1916 the ANZACs fought in modern-day Turkey against the Ottoman Empire.

The Western Front had become nothing short of a stalemate with neither side budging. Every inch of land was costing thousands of lives, the Allies needed to change something. So the momentum of the war would be decided by the performance of the soldiers in Gallipoli. The plan was to seize north western Turkey to allow arms movement between the West and Russia. The Dardanelles strait was the target and if they took them, they knew they could tip the balance of the war. The naval invasion on the shores of Gallipoli went ahead.

It began with British and French ships bombarding the coast. However, the Ottomans had a trick up their sleeve - they had placed mines in the sea, so when Allied ships entered the straits to invade, the combination of mines and Ottoman fire from the shore sunk three battleships and severely damaged three others. The British had brought old battleships, which didn't stand much chance against the land based guns. So the naval attack was a fail. This prompted the Allies to take to the land and an amphibious assault began on the shores of Gallipoli. It seemed they felt their hand was forced and they decided to continue anyway. It was poor leadership.

Men of all nationalities flooded onto the Turkish

beaches. Again the Allies lacked the right equipment to pull off this offensive. As the men landed, they were mown down. The first day saw vast numbers dead but, by the end of that first day, the Allies had secured beachheads in Cape Helles. The ANZAC force had landed to the north, missing their planned landing spot. They actually landed in a small bay which would go on to be called ANZAC Cove. The Aussies and Kiwis fought a tough, entrenched Ottoman enemy. They fought tooth and nail, yet a stalemate developed. Bodies stacked on bodies, their rotting corpses bringing flies and disease. Snipers picked off people at ground level while planes struck from the air.

The British decided to send support to the ANZACs. But slow and hesitant decision making allowed the Ottomans to wipe out the new reinforcements as they arrived. The brave ANZAC soldiers were fighting on their own. They continued to attack, relentlessly, but to no avail. Months of hard-fought warfare ensued yet still the Ottomans held the high ground.

With no help coming, and losses mounting, evacuation was the only choice but it seemed impossible to execute. The enemy held the high ground and had control of the air. So it seemed the evacuation would be like the rest of the campaign - brave soldiers, let down by poor equipment and poor decisions by those in command. However, in reality the evacuation was a stroke of genius. The Allies hid all signs of withdrawal from the Ottomans, right until the final moment where the last soldiers left. This stopped the Ottomans bombing the beach and killing hundreds or thousands. The Gallipoli campaign had been comprised of mistake after mistake with regards to leadership. The expression "lions, led by donkeys" was completely apt.

However, this plan was brilliant. The ANZAC soldiers were peeled away layer by layer until, by the last day, only those who were holding the front line were left. There were no signs of a retreat, indeed all seemed totally normal. In the weeks before the withdrawal, the Allies went long periods of being completely silent so that, when they actually left and it was quiet, it was not unusual. When the first silences had taken place, the Ottomans sent soldiers to test their defences. They were mown down. So when the ANZACs went silent on the last day of the retreat, the Ottomans didn't feel it wise to investigate just another quiet patch. Hence, over a period of 12 days, men were gradually picked up at night until 83,048 men escaped the perilous Turkish shores. So while the campaign overall had failed (and around 250,000 Allied soldiers died), the retreat was a stunning success with not one soldier killed. It turned an embarrassing military defeat into a heroic survival story.

This event would mould the New Zealand identity and have a profound effect on their development as an emerging independent nation. New Zealand was a young country and had gone through a trial by fire. This war was an alien affair - on the other side of the world, in places many had never heard of – but it would help forge a nation.

But what about the Maori? The World War had been called a "white man's war" and many Maori opposed it due to the previous harsh land confiscations and the fact that the European war had nothing to do with them. They argued that they did not share the problems of the British. However, a majority of the Maori started to show the first real signs of moving beyond old wounds. Many young Maori men wanted to fight and New Zealand ended up with 2,227 Maori (and 458 Pacific Islanders) serving in the war. 360 of those men died. To us, this may seem very strange, given the atrocities inflicted on them since the 1840 signing of the treaty of Waitangi. The Maoris had lost so much that to then fight for their enemy seems bizarre. Perhaps the explanation is that the Maori were (still are?) a warrior people, and the past 100 years had seen them lose more battles than they had won. Perhaps they just wanted to avenge these losses? Perhaps they just felt it was the morally right thing to do? Anyway, for whatever reason, many Maoris volunteered. To be clear, they were not forced to fight as Maoris weren't conscripted for the majority of the war (in contrast to white men).

So the Maori fought in all the campaigns the white New Zealanders fought. Their culture and fierce warrior spirit were not lost on the rest of New Zealand, and it inspired many Kiwis. Stories of Maori heroism circulated, such as at the battle of Chunuk Bair during the

Gallipoli campaign. This was actually the first battle these Maori men took part in. The Maori had been pinned down under Ottoman fire for some time. In need of some sort of relief, they attached bayonets and charged the Ottoman trenches, running into the fire of Ottoman guns while shouting their traditional Haka. Surprisingly few died – 17 men. The Maori had been bold, brave and heroic, and they captured the trench. They were proving their warrior ability. One British officer described the Maori as the fiercest fighters at Gallipoli. Such bravery and commitment, fighting for a nation that had treated your people so poorly, began to change opinions back in New Zealand. The fact they were fighting side by side with whites, both groups fighting for New Zealand, changed attitudes in the still segregated New Zealand. Unlike the Aboriginals who were rejected for their race, the Maori fought alongside their white counterparts.

A Maori carving in a New Zealand Trench at Gallipoli.

Race relations between whites and Maori in New Zealand at the time had been one of social division with both sides disliking the other. One example was a smallpox outbreak in 1913 where the white governing classes discriminated fairly directly against Maoris. In the media, whites were presented as superior and the Maoris as less able than whites. There was institution-alised racism in schools – with many Maori schools only teaching agricultural studies, on the basis that was what they would grow up to do – ie. manual labour. The Maori language was not taught in school, and thus many Maori became very well-spoken in English. The war proved to both sides that whites and Maori had more in common than their differences and many Maori and white men became close friends during the war. This friendship and respect would continue afterwards back at home. Indeed, even today, there is still clearly real pride about the ANZAC contribution at Gallipoli in both New Zealand and Australia. The Maori played a full part in that campaign. This involvement and the respect between the whites and the Maori is clearly shown by some of the recruitment posters around New Zealand.

'The War-Dog of New Zealand', A World War I
recruitment poster

The poster above shows a snarling British Bulldog with
Maori face tattoos along with a 'Hei Tiki' hung around
its neck. This is a good luck charm and a symbol for
loyalty, intellect and perceptiveness but potentially
most importantly symbolises that the wearer's strength
is in their character. The Dog is also stood on both a
New Zealand and British flag, showing his allegiance to
both. This poster was placed around New Zealand and

also made into a postcard, showing how respected the Maori were for their warrior nature.

Members of the World War I Maori Pioneer Battalion taking a break from trench improvement work near Gommecourt, France. Photograph taken by Henry Armytage Sanders on the 25th of July, 1918.

Following the war, there were not enough ships to take all the New Zealand troops home. So, in the meantime, some were posted in Bulford, England at Sling Camp. There, with too much spare time now the war was over, they dug a huge chalk kiwi into the side of the hill over-looking the town. This is where the nickname "the Kiwis" first became widely acknowledged and recognised.

KIWI Emblem cut out of Chalk by the N.Z. Forces to commemorate their occupation of Sling Camp, Bulford, during the Great War. The Body covers an area of 1½ acres. Height 420 ft. length of Bill 150 ft. Height of letters N.Z. 65 ft. Total area enclosed 4½ acres. The Emblem has been registered as a Military Encroachment by the Imperial Authorities and on behalf of the N.Z. Forces, its maintenance has been undertaken by the KIWI POLISH CO. Pty. Ltd., London.

A picture of Sling Camp at Bulford with the giant kiwi in the side of the hill. The Kiwi is there today. Also known as 'The Bulford Kiwi'.

Many Maoris suffered in the worldwide economic collapse of the Great Depression. The Maori farmers were the first to feel this hardship as their income fell, and many Maori lost their jobs. In the business sectors, Maoris were often first to be fired. Indeed, one survey reported that by 1933, 40% of New Zealand's unemployed were Maori. To make things worse, the Maori did not receive the same types of benefits and financial aid as the whites. This was also a time across the world of political radicalisation. The Great Depression in Europe gave the perfect platform for the rise of the Nazis, and although New Zealand did see some more radical movements - like the growth of the Communist farmers - all in all, they kept their heads and managed the problem without scapegoating and causing further social divides.

One racially driven group formed. They were called the White New Zealand League, and as you can probably guess, they weren't the nicest of fellas. Despite their malign efforts, society was beginning to move in the right direction. In 1935, the legitimacy of the problems faced by the Maoris was acknowledged by the newly elected Labour Government. They ensured that benefits would be equally distributed and the new government boosted the agricultural sector through various schemes. This disproportionately helped the Maori to get employment and to become financially stronger. This government completely changed the position the Maori in New Zealand society. Social security allowed the Maori to build funds and thus engage with white society as they hadn't before. The new government also removed all barriers to Maoris securing pensions and financial aid for children and so reduced the poverty that had really divided whites and the Maori up to this point in time. Coupled with the growth of Maori political engagement, these developments further brought them into the political picture.

The Great Depression could have easily heightened the divides between Maori and whites. Yet New Zealand somehow came out of this turbulent period more united than ever. Before this, the Maori had been peripheral to the very British dominated (with 95% of whites being British) society. This period saw the historic divisions between Maori and whites starting to dissipate as they came together as New Zealanders, or (as they are nicknamed) Kiwis.

So, in comparison to many countries (eg. blacks in South Africa or Aboriginals in Australia), New Zealand avoided the fierce animosity to its native people. Racial relations across the entire world were tense and would continue to be for the rest of the century. They scarred many nations. Let's not get ahead of ourselves, race was still a significant factor in New Zealand society at this point. White women hardly ever married Maori men, and society was in many ways a de facto segregation. However, things would get better for the Maori with the arrival of another global conflict

World War II

World War II was, in many ways, like the first world war. New Zealand dove headfirst into support for Britain and the allies. The feeling was that if Britain is in trouble then so are we. The bond was still very close. So on 3rd September 1939, New Zealand joined the most significant conflict the world has ever seen. During the war the Maori again demonstrated how fierce they are on the battlefield. However, this time they did it with more independence, getting their own battalion. Whereas in WWI their involvement had not been entirely accepted, in WWII, they became fully involved in the war effort on an equal basis.

Furthermore, rather than some Maoris still resenting the whites, most were eager to fight and wanted their own battalion. Ngata, a powerful Maori politician at the time, demanded the Maoris be allowed to fight as they were under the same laws and rule as the whites. He demonstrated this completely unconditional support for the whites when he said: "if out Pakeha brothers fall, we fall with them". [Pakeha, by the way, is the name of the Europeans in Maori]. He rallied Maori support and galvanised many Maori and whites to come together as New Zealanders. This further consolidated the Maori gains through the new laws protecting and helping them by effectively saying that, if they were to be equal to the whites, they had to fight the same war as them. The minority indigenous populations of other countries were rarely involved on the frontline. Actually fighting side by side with white kiwis was a massive statement in regards to race relations between whites and Maori. It showed a future of equality rather than division.

The Maori battalion was organised by different tribes, serving all over the globe, but mainly around the Mediterranean, seeing battle in Greece, North Africa and Italy. The memory of the Gallipoli campaign was still vivid in many people's memory and the battalion would stun many with its bravery and sheers relentlessness. Maori started to become officers which was a challenge – to learn the relevant mechanics and leadership skills since they mostly came from rural backgrounds, working on farms and in agriculture generally. They learnt the needed drills and tactics quickly, building their training on their warrior and war savvy culture, outdoing many white battalions. Indeed, their training was not limited to home soil - they went to train in the UK, where King George VI applauded their strength and battle-hungry attitude.

After this impressive training, they headed for war, deploying to Egypt, where the most difficult problem was disease. After this uneventful time, they were relocated to Greece to ensure that the invading Nazis didn't get their hands on it. Along with British and Australian soldiers and many other New Zealander soldiers, they were on the front line in northern Greece. The Nazis proved strong, and the Maori were ordered to drop back. As they retreated they left traps hoping to slow the Nazi advance. Once in Athens, the battalion was evacuated after suffering 102 casualties.

Having lost northern Greece they moved south to Crete, where their fierce warrior reputation was confirmed. They formed a garrison to defend the island's shores. The island had been the place of the mythological mino-taur, and would again see the stuff of legends. The Maori had the task of defending on of the islands main airfields. The Allied troops knew that a German offen-sive would come, they just didn't know when, where or how. But British leadership actually did know. The man in charge of the Allies forces on Crete was Bernard Frey-berg. He had actually knew (thanks to British intel) when and where the invasion would come. He told the troops nothing and on the morning of the invasion he is reported to have said "they're right on time". The Maori troops on the ground were stunned.

The Germans knew that, to win a land battle, first you had to neutralise the air force. So, on 20th May 1941, the Germans attacked the main airfield defended by the Maori. The attack was huge – with German para-troopers parachuting down to complement German land soldiers landing on various beaches. The battle raged across the island. Fighting was chaotic with the defenders not knowing where the enemy was, having landed all around them. One example was when Maori troops found a house with 18 Germans inside. The Maori slowly gained the upper hand and killed eight of the Germans before the rest surrendered. However, the Germans kept coming. The island soon became full of both German and Allied soldiers. The battle for Crete was in full flow and the Maori again punched above their weight. The Battalion's motto was "Ake! Ake! Kia Kaha E!" ("Upwards, Upwards, Be strong!").

Another time, on their way to reinforce another unit of Kiwis, the Maori Battalion encountered a Nazi platoon. The Maori forced them to surrender, granting them mercy. However, one Nazi thought it wise to chuck a grenade at them while surrendering. The Maori response was to fix bayonets to their rifles, charge the Nazis, and killed all 24. This aggressive style of war was repeated on other occasions, where they charged the enemy with their bayonets. From such events, the Maori were talked about in German camps, getting nicknamed the knifemen and reinforcing their warrior reputation. Some Nazis started to fear this unknown illusive Maori force. However, the heroics of the Maori could not keep the German war machine at bay. Their conquest of Crete looked inevitable so the Allies prepared to evacuate. During the evacuation of Crete, the Maori volunteered to stay to guard the withdrawal, protecting the other soldiers while they fled. For days they defended the port of Sfakia. The Maori battalion saw 243 casualties while fighting in a last stand to protect the evacuation, until they too left.

A Maori soldier after escaping Greece and making it to Alexandria. Taken in 1941.

Following this campaign, the Maori went back to Egypt, performing the Haka for the camp. However, the relative quiet did not last, as they soon found themselves up against tanks in the dry arid deserts of Libya. Their reputation preceded them – as the stories of them slaughtering Nazi soldiers in Crete with bayonets had made their way to Nazi officers in Libya. The Maori continued their now-famous bayonet charge tactics, becoming known as "scalp hunters" across northern Africa. Even the highest German officers heard of them, including Rommel, who led the German North Africa campaign. In Libya, the fighting was hard-fought, comprised of fights spreading across miles of sand but focused on small built-up rocky trenches.

Members of the Maori Battalion performing the Haka while posted in Egypt. The man at the front is Te Kooti Reihana, the three men behind him were all killed in the war. Only the soldier at the front would return home. Following the war, he fell into alcoholism and struggled. This was the unfortunate fate of many of those returning from war.

One story emerged from the Libya campaign of a group of Maori soldiers who had pushed too far into enemy territory, and found themselves surrounded by Italian troops. Pinned down, it seemed that they had finally met their match and it would take nothing short of a miracle to save the Battalion. A young Maori private, called Charles Shelford, got up amidst the relentless fire from the Italian guns and charged towards one of their trenches. Firing as he ran, he was hit by a grenade, fragments exploded into his legs. He scrambled to find a grenade of his own, and he threw it into the Italian trench. This caused so much damage that the Italian force was now confused and ultimately surrendered. This brave young Maori survived the war, winning the Distinguished Conduct Medal. The North Africa campaign is full of such heroic stories.

A Maori soldier servicing his rifle. May 1943, Tunis, North Africa.

As the battle for North Africa roared on, the Maori moved into Tunisia. The Maori were on the front line fighting the Axis powers. In 1943 as the war was in the balance, the Maori Battalion was ordered to take the Tebaga Gap, an important strategic location giving access to both Tunisia's coast and inland, cutting through the mountainous terrain. The various surrounding hills were divided between German and Allied possession. The Maori Battalion had the role of taking a hill called Point 209. One Maori really did play a heroic part in seizing this objective. Moana-Nui-a-Ki wa Ngarimu led the offensive. A German Panzer division was deployed at the summit of the hill. A panzer, by the way, is a German tank. A good one too. The tank was one of the main reasons Germany was able to steamroll through France at the beginning of the war. It seemed the Maori were being asked to lay down their lives on a mission that would probably fail and even if it was won, the cost would be great.

So, the Maori troops began the trek up the rocky, dry hills. It was quiet. As they climbed, they expected to see signs of the Germans but nothing. Indeed, they got to the top of the hill and Ngarimu claimed it for the Allies. However, there was a slight problem – this was not Point 209, but a false summit on the route up to a much larger hill. They were only halfway there. So they carried on and then he saw the Germans. Or more importantly, the Germans saw the Maori and opened fire on the upcoming Maoris. Two machine guns covered the hillside with a rain of bullets while mortar bombs landed among the attacking Maori. Ngarimu somehow kept his troops going. He was at the front, leading the charge, and indeed leading by example. He shot both of the machine gunners himself. Thus the

Maori could climb without the constant threat of being mowed down. After more fighting, the Germans retreated enabling Ngarimu and the Maori Battalion to take Point 209.

However, the Germans had only retreated so that they could counter-attack with a far greater force. Ngarimu knew they would be back and got his troops to dig deep manholes for the soldiers to fight from. This would reduce the impact of machine-gun fire and mortars. Ngarimu's tactics were superb, allowing the Maori to pick off the approaching Germans. Ngarimu killed many himself, getting shot in the shoulder to go with the shrapnel in his leg. His men urged him to go for treatment, but he refused, insisting he stay with them on the battlefield. The battle continued into the night, with both sides dug into the hill. Neither budging, simply killing their enemy if they tried to advance.

Suddenly, Ngarimu saw a weakness in the German line. He rushed into it, firing his Tommy gun as he charged. The Germans were surprised and many were killed by this one man tornado. When he ran out of ammo, and now in enemy territory, he threw rocks to keep the Germans pinned down, as his troops joined him.

Through the night, he kept morale high despite the relentless bloodshed. The Germans counter-attacked again and forced the Maori back to their old positions. But they held firm at the top of the hill. Finally, morning came and Ngarimu died as the sun rose in Africa and as it set in New Zealand, in his homeland of Aotearoa. He was awarded the Victoria Cross, for his bravery, leadership and for making the ultimate sacrifice. To be so fearless in death and to know that you will die requires something I am unable to understand. It is courage beyond belief and it is compassion for his men above all else. His fearlessness in death is probably best summed up by Marcus Aurelius when he said "Death smiles at us all, all a man can do is smile back"

Photo of Moana-Nui-a-Ki wa Ngarimu, taken in 1940

The Maoris stayed in Tunisia to combat the Italians where they besieged heavily fortified bases. This campaign saw significant Maori losses. In one single battle, fighting over a monastery surrounded by hilly, dry and sandy terrain, there were 128 Allied casualties, many of which were Maoris. Eventually the cumulative damage to the Maori force left them unable to fight on the front line for a considerable time. However, the "scalp hunters" were not entirely finished – as they joined other Allied units to help push the Nazis back in northern Italy. Overall, 3,600 men fought in the Maori battalion, ¾ of those who signed up would never see the shores of New Zealand again. These Maori warriors sacrificed much in the fight against Fascism and oppression, and also for the progress of their people in New Zealand. The Maori Battalion was the most decorated of all the New Zealand active service units and seems to have caused a disproportionate amount of damage to the Nazis and Italians.

Concurrently, New Zealand was facing the threat from Japan to the north. While Japan never attempted to invade - there just wasn't much to gain from taking the two Islands with little in the way of the resources they needed, i.e. oil, tin, rubber, steel, coal etc. However, New Zealand was involved in the Pacific conflict, mainly supporting the U.S. forces. Much of the Kiwi air force had been stationed in Malaya and had been destroyed by the Japanese. However, they rebuilt and, towards the end of the war, ANZAF (like the ANZAC but for Air Force) they grew in size and bombed several Japanese bases. The Kiwi army did some island hopping but was ultimately following in the footsteps of the US. Obviously, there is much more to the story of New Zealand in the Pacific, but for the Maoris, Europe was their main battleground.

So, as I hope you have appreciated, the Second World

War was pivotal in the growth of Maori in New Zealand society. Maori were taking leadership positions for the first time, and there was more talk of Maori and whites being one people. The Maoris population had been increasing before the war and continued to do so. Unlike many native populations, the Maori weren't going to disappear. A new national identity was forming.

Domestically, the war had left many jobs unfilled jobs as the men had gone off to war. The Maori took several of these, finding work in the cities and thus moving into the urban areas, causing the two races to live in closer proximity to one another. Many Maori viewed the war as "the price of citizenship" and fully integrated into New Zealand society. Until World War II, the two groups were almost viewed as separate nations. Afterwards, however, in 1947 New Zealand claimed independence from Britain, so that now people were no longer British or Maori but rather were New Zealanders.

Soon after WWII, New Zealand was involved in fighting the Communist uprising in Malaya, who were fighting to overthrow British rule. New Zealand, being in the Commonwealth, was quick to come to help Britain. My Grandfather served for the British army in Malaya, as part of his national service. In 1952, Grampy got the call up. He distinctly remembers getting paid twenty four shillings a week, ie. £1.20 a week!!! Anyways, after six weeks of training he was asked where he wanted to be stationed. I asked him about his time in national service and he told me: "I asked to rejoin the Northants regiment who were in Germany as my first choice but was amazed to find I was assigned to join the East Yorkshire Regiment and to go to Malaya for two years!". So a few weeks later he found himself aboard the HMT Empire Clyde headed for Malaya. By pure chance this was the very ship that had evacuated the Maori troops from Crete to Egypt in World War II as they fled the German invasion. The thought that my Grandfather was on the same ship as those Maori 'Scalp Hunter' soldiers a mere ten years later is a weird one, and it is the only, tenuous, link I have to the Maori.

Anyways, Grampy was headed for Malaya, via the Bay of Biscay and Egypt (which was the first stop en route to Malaya). At Suez he said: "we saw lots of bumboats round the ship trying to sell trinkets and boys were diving for whatever coins we threw down. I remember the gully-gully man coming aboard to do amazing tricks for our entertainment and then it was through the Suez Canal to Aden." The next stop was Colombo in Sri Lanka and from there to Singapore and hence Malaya. Anyways, back to the Maori.

Although the Maori had proved themselves as New Zealanders in the Second World War; politically they were still second class (for instance, they voted on a different day to whites). In the 1950's this all changed. Maori political representation had been granted in the 1800's, following the New Zealand wars, but this was still segmented – with special seats reserved for Maoris. During the second half of the 20th century these distinctions changed – for instance in 1967, Maoris were allowed to run for white seats. Later, Maori only seats were abolished – only to be re-established in the 1990's (to ensure Maori representation).

Additionally, during the 1960's and 70's there were various protests, demanding the government address stolen land and other social and economic disparities. In response to this various affirmative action policies were put in place by the government. The divide in relation to socioeconomic prosperity continued to narrow.

Throughout the latter half of the century, the Maori

population continued to grow, reaching 300,000 in 1980. The increase in headcount was reflected in growing political power. Now policy formation started to take Maori needs into account. During this period, the treaty of Waitangi posed a significant point of debate, with many Maori wanting land to be returned. However, this stayed a minority view and the Maori and whites became closer, coming together to form the dynamic we have today. Furthermore, socially, whites and Maoris began to marry far more often, and this helped to continue to close the social divide. Indeed, this togetherness and anti-segregation stance was demonstrated in the vast and widescale protests against apartheid during the 1981 tour by the South African national rugby team, the Springboks.

The kind, humble and friendly nature of New Zealand was first illustrated to me by Kane Williamson. He is captain of the New Zealand national cricket team, the "Black Caps". I was lucky enough to go to the cricket world cup final in 2019 at Lords. It was England vs New Zealand. I was with my dad, Mr. Pedley, my grandfather (Grampy), my god brother (Will) and a good mate's dad (Chaz). The world cup had been great entertainment but the final took it to another level. If you don't like cricket maybe skip this part.

For the whole day, neither side managed to achieve dominance with the balance favouring one team and then the other. By the end, after looking dominant and then looking down and out, it was a monumental innings from Ben Stokes for England that drew the game after the 50 overs. Unbelievable. It had never happened before. A "Super over" was next - each side having 6 balls to hit as many runs as possible. Nail-biting stuff. England hit 15 runs off their 6 balls. New Zealand hit 14 runs with one ball left - 2 runs would win the world cup. Martin Guptill, the batsman, slams the ball along the floor. The kiwi batsmen sprint for the runs. They make one and turn for the second as Jason Roy collects the ball and fires it back to the wicket-keeper, Jos Buttler. Guptill is quick. The ball is quicker and gets to Buttler's hands while Guptill is still metres away from World Cup glory. Buttler demolishes the stumps and Guptill is run out. The scores are level and no-one really knew who had won.

It turns out that England had won on the basis they had hit more boundaries during the 50 overs. Potentially the most unjust way possible to win a world cup. New Zealand must have felt completely robbed. They had tied. So surely there should be another Super over to see who wins. But no. England lifts the world cup and New Zealand must travel home across the world, losers. The Kiwi captain, Kane Williamson, had been the player of the entire tournament, and was interviewed after the game. He did not complain at all, he congratulated England, said thank you for a fantastic world cup and said he was proud of his team. I was gobsmacked at how gracious he was in such an unjust defeat and showed me so much about New Zealanders – that they fight hard, but do not complain and respect their opponents. They are gracious in both victory and defeat, treating "both these imposters just the same". I think this attribute explains why the whites and Maori are so intertwined today. They have so much respect for one another and do not let bitterness, jealousy or defeat cloud their minds.

Anyways back to the history. In 1987, New Zealand began disarmament, declaring themselves a nuclear weapon-free zone. Despite their war oriented past, post-WW2 their identity changed to a more progressive and peaceful nature. In many ways, the New Zealand whites have always been liberal when compared to other British colonial countries. The Maori as a minority population has fared far better than the blacks in South Africa or the Aboriginals in Australia.

Coexistence has now been entrenched into New Zealand society. The two peoples have been socially intertwined for over a century and the "Kiwi" identity has become a co-joined lifestyle – with each people adopting one another's cultures. For example, the New Zealand national rugby team performs the Haka every time they play, and it has become a trademark both for the country and for the sport of rugby. The Maori and their rugby success are similar to the fairytale story of the Jamaican sprinters, so rarely has a small population been able to dominate a worldwide sport quite so intensely.

New Zealand, for us in Britain or America, feels distant and disconnected. Indeed even today, New Zealand is sometimes left off world maps. New Zealanders see the funny side on this - if you go to their government error page where it says "404 error not found", they have a world map that doesn't include New Zealand on it.

Although New Zealand is indeed very far away from most of the rest of the world, its history is intertwined with many countries. Indeed, it has become apparent to me that I am writing about three places that all feel a bit distant from our day to day life. Perhaps that's the point - it helps us better understand ourselves when we look at distant places and try to distill the lessons from their past.

Throughout the history of New Zealand, the whites seem to have respected the warrior nature of the Maori. The Maori seem to have returned that respect. Indeed, perhaps this mutual respect has been the difference in racial history compared to other colonised countries. The Maoris saw many things to be gained from white immigration, whether it be muskets (historically) or jobs in the cities (more recently). They now coexist and both peoples seem to have gained from their relation-ship and are now far stronger together than apart.

PART III

THE FRENCH-CANADIANS

CANADA

The Beginning

So let's start at the end. The year is 1995. Quebec, Canada's majority French-speaking province, is voting on becoming independent from Canada, where English is the major language. The French-Canadians are at a crossroads in their history. The bars are packed, living rooms full, and Quebecois rallies overflowing. The whole country is fixed on the result of the referendum. For 236 years the flags of Canada had hung over Quebec; and now the Quebecois are divided on whether to stick with Canada or go it alone. French-

Canadian Independence. How Canada and the French-Canadian people got here is a long and compelling journey. To understand their decision, one must first understand their past.

The French-Canadian people are not as distinct from their fellow countrymen as the Afrikaners and Maoris. Where the Maori and Afrikaners are divided from their fellows by race, the French-Canadians are not. Indeed, over time they and the English-Canadians have become closer, and their specific identity as a people is less pronounced in comparison to the Afrikaners and the Maori. The story of the French-Canadians is one of people who have merged into and with another people. That said, they have their own language and culture - and the identity of being French-Canadian is engraved into Quebec. Quebec is the recognised stronghold of the French-Canadians. Today, 34% (11.9 million) of Canada is French-Canadian, whereas in Quebec, 81% of the population speak French as their first language. The division of the French-Canadians with their fellow countrymen is one of language, geography and history.

But let's get back to the beginning. Before any Europeans had found their way to Canada, indigenous peoples inhabited the land. They lived from the Atlantic to the Pacific, from the Arctic to the Great Lakes. They were comprised of multiple different peoples - from the Inuits to the Cree to the Slavey people and more. It is thought that they came across the Bering Strait at a time when Asia and North America were connected by a land bridge. No one really knows when this happened, some reckon it was as much as 100,000 years ago, others think it was as little as 12,000 years ago. The point is, they've been spanning Canada for a while, and indeed went from Alaska all the way to the southernmost tip of Argentina. As they travelled, they developed technologies from snowshoes to kayaks to help them thrive in the forests and plains of the Great White North.

So Canada pre-European settlement was pretty simple. Indigenous peoples, living in tribal systems across all the land. With its big expansive plains, mountains and hundreds of lakes, cold winters but hot and dry summers on the Prairies and milder on the coast, it was prime for European settlement.

The First Europeans

The first Europeans to find their way to the Americas were the Vikings. They came from Scandinavia around the year 1000, travelling via Iceland and along the coast of Greenland, before finding themselves in Newfound-land. They settled, and signs of their settlement are still clear to see today at L'Anse aux Meadows. However, they died out. No-one is really too sure why - some think they lost ongoing battles with the natives. However, after talking to my Dad, we both think it could have been as simple as a couple of really harsh winters that polished them off. Anyway, as a result, the Americas would remain elusive to the eager European kings and queens for the next 500 years.

So it was not until 1492 that the curtain of the Atlantic Ocean and the mysteries that lay beyond it were fully drawn. Christopher Columbus had ventured into the far unknown and returned with news of a new land, which would give birth to the expansion and creation of worldwide empires. Columbus had actually landed in the Bahamas, which I know it isn't exactly Canada, but this discovery would start the European interest in the continent. The sprint for the control of the Americas had begun, and Henry VII sent John Cabot to find the land and claim it for England. Now 'John' was actually called Giovanni Caboto and he was from Genoa, but as he was working for the English, he became John Cabot.

I studied Henry VII briefly at school. I can't really remember a whole lot, but I can tell you that he was quite conservative and built up some serious wealth. For those who don't know how the story ends, his son Henry VIII spends all of it and more. I never really found Henry VII that enticing, so I'll spare you the details - all you need to know is that in 1497 he sent John Cabot to the new world to claim the land. He landed near today's Canadian / US border and claimed the surrounding coastal areas. Henry sent him off again the following year in the hope that he could claim further land. However, Cabot would not return, being added to the long list of those who would die in the search of new lands.

A few fishermen began to settle in what would become modern day Canada, but they were small (and seasonal) outposts. The rich seas off Canada were an untapped goldmine for fisherman used to the over-fished and crowded European waters. Various explorers came and went, however, no-one really consolidated any claim in these wonderful new lands.

So, I hear you ask, where are the French-Canadians? Well, they came after all the first wave of claiming was done. They may have been late to the party, but they didn't let that get in their way from taking some of the land for themselves. Jacques Cartier, in 1534, made it to Canada and claimed Canada for France. This new region had been named 'New France' or in French, 'Nouvelle-France'. It would come to be what today we know as Quebec.

Jacques Cartier, painted by Théophile Hamel Circa 1844

Cartier found a land that was utterly European in its climate and fishing. It was perfect for settlement. The land was thought to be rich in nutrients and minerals and, maybe most importantly, gold. Having been sent by Francis I, he found the Saint Lawrence River and claimed the land surrounding it for France. He made contact with the natives, kidnapping two native boys. One boy happened to be the son of the chief. They were brought back to France to show off the new discovery of Canada. Apparently, what surprised the two boys most during their time in France was not the civilised modern society, but rather the way the French raised their children. In their culture children were never hit for making mistakes, yet in France at the time beating children was typical. They also gave Canada its name, as in their language "Kanata" means settlement, this stuck and became frenchified into Canada.

Once, Francis I had heard about the riches and opportunity to be found in Canada he sent Cartier back out on a second expedition. So he crossed the Atlantic once more and navigated up the Saint Lawrence River all the way to Stadacona. On his arrival he began the first settlements of modern-day Quebec; Quebec City and Montreal. They stayed there for the winter, painfully learning that Quebec and southern France had quite different climates. Following this experience, they returned to France, where they loaded ships with men and women to populate this new colony for France. Many were prisoners who the French wanted to get off their hands. However, it was not all smooth sailing. The exotic stories told by Cartier of gold and riches turned out to be nothing more than stories. This news was a turning point – the French were gutted and lost all interest in the new settlement. It went from a place of enticing dreams of wealth to being viewed as a cold barren land with little to offer other than fishing and furs. Although 'formal' French control ended, Frenchies continued to live there, and the settlements around the Saint Lawrence River continued to get by.

So, a hundred-odd years passed until Henri IV, the king of France at the time, reinvigorated French interest. In 1598 he made it official by putting a fella by the name of Troilus de La Roche de Mesgouez in charge of Canada. Henri IV made several attempts to establish new colonies but it was only Quebec that showed signs of potential growth, prospering as a fur trading post. However, the Frenchies were not alone in North America, as the English started to show interest. They landed in Virginia in 1607. The French and English have been fighting in Europe for centuries, and it looked as though they had found a new battleground. The first problem the English posed was their interest in Acadia, a French territory. The real French worry was the potential loss of profit from the fur trading which they dominated. For the next decade, Quebec stayed as a simple trading post - the dreams of a large French colony had not yet arisen. However, as the race for land began, so too did the French desire for a large colony in Canada. Their thinking was that if they didn't take the land, the English or the Dutch would. Thus the French colonisation of Quebec began, and a man by the name of Samuel de Champlain was put in charge. In 1608 he built the foundations of settlement that would become

Quebec City. It became a more extensive trading post and prospered generally.

However, with their arrival came interaction with the indigenous people. The Frenchies and the natives started to interact. The natives craved the new technologies of Europe - they wanted rifles and the wonders of gunpowder to settle old scores against rival tribes. The French colony wanted to grow and expand, and needed the support of at least some native tribes. So Champlain agreed alliances with both the Algonquins and the Hurons. However, as they made allies, they inevitably made enemies, including the Iroquois. A century of fighting unfolded, and the Iroquoians were expelled from the region while thousands died from diseases brought over from Europe. In sum, although the Hurons defeated their enemy the Iroquois, it was only the European powers that really won the various wars with and between the native tribes.

Up until 1617, migration from France to their new colony was mainly limited to fur traders. So, although the site for settlement had been built by Champlain and his men, no-one had come over to inhabit it. That changed in 1617 when the first genuine settlers to this new colony left France for the promise of New France. The money from the fur trade in Quebec was now becoming sizeable, and seemed fairly stable as there was no real threat from the natives anymore. Many natives were converting to Christianity and integrating into the money making enterprises. French businessmen began to take an interest. A fella by the name of Cardinal Richelieu founded a company to oversee managing New France. The "Company of New France" ran the show for a while, keeping trade ticking along, retaining the French claim on the land, and running a nice profit in the process. This new-found investment in the region led to the creation of the Royal Province of New France and it seemed France would dominate northern North America with the English to the south. In 1663, the King of France (Louis XVIII) took control of the colony, nationalised the business aspects to be fully under the rule of the king. This changed the focus – from an economic / business mentality to a political / national objective. The thinking evolved to suggest that France needed to expel the natives from this New France region so their settlements could expand. And if they were to get rid of the natives, they would need an army.

Hence, in 1665, French troops landed in Quebec. 1200 colonial troops to fight the natives. The Iroquois people were outmatched - many fled and many died – and the Colonial era of domination over Canada was underway. King Louis XIV decided that, rather than bring the soldiers back to France, they should settle in New France. He promised land to those who stayed. In the end, about a third of the troops stayed, and this helped the population grew throughout the 1660s. By 1666 the population was recorded at 4,219 people. However, there was a problem – there were too few women. Most of the settlers were either soldiers or fur traders, and hence the colony couldn't grow. Many men simply could not find partners. So Louis XIV sent vast numbers of women out. These were known as the 'Filles du Roi' (ie. the King's Daughters) and this drastically changed the picture. Men now had another reason to live there - they were having families. Just seven years after the 1666 census, the population had grown almost 60% to 6,700. This paled in comparison to the 120,000 living in the English colonies to the south but showed promise. Indeed, the settlers even started to have a distinct name - New France residents became known as Canadiens or Canadois.

Women coming to Quebec in 1667, in order to be married to the French-Canadian farmers. Painted by Eleanor Fortescue-Bricklade. Painted prior to 1927.

The next 80 odd years were uneventful. New France continued to grow in size - both in population and territory. However, in 1756, this all changed, as the war in Europe came to Canada. The days of colonial discovery – and simple expansion - in North America were coming to a close. Now the fight over that territory would begin. For the past 300 years, European powers had been claiming the Americas and growing their settlements. The British had set up 13 colonies and owned Hudson Bay; France owned New France from Louisiana to Quebec right through the centre of North America. The Canadiens identity had begun to form – as a people far from home within a new uncharted land, surrounded on many sides by the perfidious Albion. The coming challenges would push them like never before.

The Seven Years war is almost a forgotten world war - it spanned five continents and every major power in Europe was involved. North America became one of the key battlegrounds. The reason for the war was depressingly familiar. Long story short there was a bit of disagreement between the European powers, which escalated and ended up with Great Britain and Prussia going to war with France and Austria. The war has taken many names. In America and Canada, it is known as the French and Indian War, in Germany, it is called the Third Silesian War, while the Swedish call it the Pomeranian War. I will be referring to it as the Seven Years war because it's easier and since the war lasted 9 years.

The North America element of the conflict began as British settlers in the 13 colonies expanded into the vast expanses of the mid-west of America. This expansion would profit the British as they gained resources and new markets. However, the French also claimed the land, even though barely anyone lived there. Frankly, the French didn't want a stronger Britain, which might get to a point where they were so strong they could take more important French colonies. The war in North America also heavily involved native Americans who, prior to the war, had been able to play off the French and British against each other.

The Seven Years war actually started in North America with a young British officer called George Washington leading the first raids into some disputed territory. He pushed over the Appalachians to fight the French. Following a number of small confrontations, the Brits decided to send thousands of troops to America, landing in Virginia and Nova Scotia. The General charged with leading the British conquest of the French territories was a Scot, Edward Braddock. George Washington became his right-hand man, and they marched into the forests in search of French forts. They searched for days, weeks and months until they came across Duquesne, which was a massive French fortification. However, French and allied native Americans had laid a trap to ambush the British. They waited in the dense forest for the British to be off guard and then they struck. The small French and Native American force tore through the British troops. So the British campaign in North America had not started as hoped - war had not even officially started and they had been defeated. Tensions were high, and on the eve of war, the French sent a further 2,600 troops to New France. The British, however, avenged their earlier defeat by beating these new French troops at Crown Point. Having won this battle, they moved to take Acadia. However, the Acadians proved tough. These Canadiens refused to back down despite being heavily outnumbered and out-armed. Gradually though, the British disbursed the Acadians, removing them from the continent. However, a core of Canadiens remained in Quebec City and Montreal.

The future of these French people would be decided by the outcome of this war. In effect, deciding if they will rule or be ruled. The British continued to send armies to North America as did the French. The French stronghold of Quebec was the only real threat to overall British dominance. The French sent a new General by the name of Montcalm, who was quick to mobilise. He took the region around the Great Lakes. The British responded by sending even more troops but the tough Frenchies continued to hold off the British attacks. These people would become the forefathers of the French-Canadian people and they fought heroically to establish their liberty.

The native community continued to help the French. When the British attacked the French forts, the natives launched counter-strikes. By now, the war was in full flow, raging across the whole of the northern half of North America. A total war - from the oceans to the forests, from the mountains to the grasslands. For the natives, the war was one of survival and ruthless killing. They had a completely different understanding of warfare to the Europeans. General Montcalm had brought the war into a sort of balance. In effect he laid the foundations for the French-Canadian identity. He brought the French to a position where they could even win the war in America. However, the British elected a new Prime Minister, William Pitt, who knew that winning North America could mean winning the war in Europe. So he invested in the North American war effort, sending more troops and, perhaps more importantly, moving much of the British Navy into the Atlantic. They positioned along the North American shoreline to prevent French resupplies and troops from entering. Until now, Montcalm had had the full extent of the French military behind him; however, now he would have to work with what he had. Britain had changed the rules and tipped the scales. Those in New France were now isolated. To make things worse for Montcalm, the harvest was poor, and thus his troops began to go hungry. Hunger broke the French camp, and leaders started to disagreed on tactics. They were now effectively trapped by the British. With Britain ruling the seas, by 1758 British victories began to come thick and fast - the heartland of America was falling to them, along with the coastline of Canada. Montcalm was able to win a battle (at Ticonderoga), however, the future of the war looked grim for the isolated French. After the British had taken Nova Scotia, they set their sights on Quebec.

The French presence in North America and their own self rule would be decided in Quebec. A confrontation of the main armies of both sides. The British brought in another 8,500 men along with General James Wolfe. Taking Quebec was his clear goal. If he took Quebec, the

British would own North America. If he lost, the French would probably be able to turn the tide of the war. Wolfe was young yet in poor health, but he had an incredible track record - an ability to somehow find victory in the hardest of circumstances. Montcalm had proved his mettle and his resilience. Both were mavericks in their own right.

Montcalm heard news of Wolfe's advance on Quebec City as supply ships had witnessed the British army on their arrival. Montcalm's right-hand man, Vaudreuil was so confident that the British wouldn't get up the river that he had not bothered to send troops to patrol the area. Navigating the river for the British would be near impossible as they had no pilots. Pilots were needed to take ships up and down the river, traversing the currents. However, the British Navy managed to do just this, largely thanks to the genius of James Cook, who would soon discover much of the Pacific along with Denis Vitre, a Canadian renegade. The French, shocked by the news, sent their fleet to engage the British but other British ships in the area were able to intercept them and so prevented any engagement with the main British fleet.

Wolfe set up base in Ile D'Orleans as it was undefended and near the city. One of Wolfe's generals, Monckton, took much of the artillery up a large hill outside the city. For weeks, the guns battered the city. In spite of this, the battle would prove very hard. Montcalm had fortified Quebec City well. Although Wolfe had taken much of the neighbouring land, Quebec City held firm. Wolfe's hope had been to force Montcalm to come out and fight as the damage to the city would be too great. But no such luck so Wolfe went to attack at Montmorency Falls at Bowport. The fight was a disaster for the British. The French confidently repulsed them. It looked as though the British effort for Quebec had failed and the war would continue. It looked like the full might of the British Empire had been blunted by New France.

However, on September 13th 1759, Wolfe decided to have one last go at it. His new plan was bold and almost unthinkable. It seemed impossible, suicide even. Wolfe took his army in several small boats in the middle of the night. They floated down the river to the bottom of the steepest cliff (half of Quebec is built on a cliff). By sheer luck or brilliance, they found they were able to climb it. The French had deemed it impossible for an army to approach that way and therefore left it relatively undefended. Undetected, the British scaled the cliffs. The cliff turned red in the night from the red jackets of the British soldiers. Hundreds climbed. None spoke. In complete silence, the British ascended into the heights of Quebec.

As the first soldiers reached the top, a French soldier heard the noises of the men climbing. He became concerned, drew his rifle, suspecting enemies. He shouted - "Who's there?". The British froze. Halfway up a cliff face and the enemy had heard them. But then a British soldier called Donald Macdonald replied in perfect French - 'Francais'. It went quiet. If discovered the British would either fall to their deaths or be gunned down. The seconds felt like hours. The defender replied, suspecting nothing. He had bought it. Wolfe had purposely put French-speaking troops at the top in case of such an encounter and the British made their way onto the top of the hill. They took the top of the cliff.

In the morning, as the sun rose upon New France's diamond city, it was the British looking down on it. They stood on what would become known as the Plains of Abraham, named after the French farmer who owned the field. The British were unopposed and headed for the city. The British artillery under Wolfe was impeccable, and the battle ahead would show just that. In training, when his men made mistakes, rather than whip them (like most Generals did at the time), he made them dress up in women's clothing and parade around the camp. He ensured his men were trained to the highest level before the battle.

A Scotsman was the first to tell Montcalm that the British were on the Plains of Abraham. Montcalm asked the man if he was drunk. He dismissed him and thought nothing of it until some Frenchies told him the same impossible story. Montcalm could not believe it and realised he had been outsmarted and outmanoeuvred by Wolfe. He hurried his army to the Plains of Abraham. There was still a battle to be fought - Wolfe was effectively cornered on the edge of a cliff. As the

French approached, the British shifted their troops into a line stretching over a mile long. The French advanced, firing as they did so. From over 120 metres most bullets missed. The British remained calm and stood firm. Montcalm was advancing his troops without reinforcements. The French advance continued and Wolfe was hit twice by the French gunfire. Yet he stayed on the battlefield. Already sick and now wounded, he stayed with his men. When about 40 metres apart, Wolfe ordered the British to open fire. This quick and devastating firing stunned the French, who stopped advancing, and then started retreating, back to Bowport (the site of the previous British defeat).

In the battle, Wolfe endured a final shot to the chest. He had led the British to glory in spite of being in poor health for the entirety of the Quebec campaign. As the British advanced and took the city of Quebec, Wolfe was bleeding slowly to his death. A British soldier found him and told him of the victory and how the French had retreated. His last words were "Now, God be praised, I will die in peace". General Montcalm was also wounded and died the following day in Quebec City. So the two great generals who had forged Canadian history died together. Both men had fought valiantly for their country, for their people and for their own personal pride. General Wolfe is often referred to as 'lucky', and fortune may have been on his side, but without his meticulous preparation and his bravery to attempt the impossible there would have been no victory.

'Death of General Wolfe' by Benjamin West

At school, Mr Pedley taught me about this war and the personal confrontation between Montcalm and Wolfe. He highlighted the bravery of both sides and drew out Wolfe as a man wanting to die in the glory of battle rather than from a slow lingering sickness. He explained the stages of the battle of the Plains of Abraham, and the blackboard slowly developed into this grand portrayal of the key encounter of the Seven Years war in North America. The whole class was gripped by the way he combined the wide historic story telling with personalisation of the main protagonists. For instance, when Wolfe was first made head of the British army in Canada, the Duke of Newfoundland was furious. He described Wolfe as "strange" and with "unusual behaviours". Wolfe was tall and lanky and refused to wear a wig. He was an outsider who had never led an army before, so one can see why they doubted him. Wolfe was unique in his methods. When the King heard him described as mad by the Duke of Newfoundland, he is reported to have said – "I hope he makes my other generals mad too!"

One of the regiments that fought with General Wolfe was the East Yorkshire regiment, in which my Grandfather would serve some 200 years later. When my Grandfather was called up for his national service in 1952 he went to the Quebec Barracks in Northampton-shire. These barracks are of course named in honour of the Quebec campaign and the battle for Quebec City. The East Yorkshire regiment's logo was a white rose, however it incorporated the white rose being surrounded in black to honour the death of General Wolfe at the battle of the Plains of Abraham. Grampy is full of bizarre yet brilliant facts, I remember revising for my GCSE history exam at his house. He told me about the Cold War and how he was sent down to Malaya to help prevent a communist revolution. He told me lots of useful things but what I remember most is him telling me how some of the best rubber in the world comes from that neck of the woods. He worked in the shoe making business for decades so I could under-stand his excitement. Anyways, back on topic.

Following the battle, Quebec City fell, and New France fell with it. In 1763, at the treaty of Paris, New France formally became part of the British Empire. The war was over, and the French-Canadian people would be confronted with the problem of British rule. This was the beginning of an all British Canada. To add insult to injury to these plucky French-Canadians, many in France seemed not to care about New France. Voltaire, a famous French philosopher and writer, when referring to Canada, stated: "it was just a few acres of snow". This complete abandonment by France left the French-Canadian people to find their own identity.

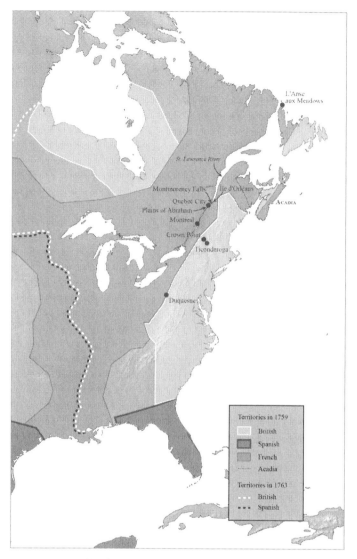

North America during the Seven Years War

It wasn't long until war raged again in North America. This time it was further south. The American War of Independence or, as it is known in America, the American Revolution, saw the 13 British colonies fight for their independence. For Canada, which didn't formally exist yet, there was little in common with the 13 colonies. Indeed, the French-Canadians, centred in Quebec, had little to gain from the war. They were moving away from identifying as French people, to be more Canadiens and Quebecers. Also, the war was about the rights of Englishmen in North America, and the Canadiens weren't English, so they didn't share this same feeling of entitlement to rights within the Empire. They felt like subjects.

Furthermore, in 1774 the Quebec Act was passed, and it made Quebec larger. It also gave higher levels of autonomy and established provisional rule of Quebec by their own legislative body. This was creating a sense of self-determination, along with more prosperity arising from the association with the British Empire, which provided access to world markets along with overall protection. So, even when the French got involved in the war, aiding the American Rebels, the Quebec population stuck with Great Britain. The days of being French were over. They felt neither British or French, unlike the other English folks in the Canadian colonies.

But the French-Canadians were not unaffected by the war further south. British loyalists who weren't happy with the independence movement moved up to Canada and Quebec. It changed the dynamic, bringing in more English people. They began to greatly outnumber the French-Canadians. Tensions between the two groups started to rise.

Meanwhile, over in Europe, the French Revolution took place. Many fled France to North America for the freedom and economic opportunity. One example of this was the Bousquette family (who are personal friends of mine, family even). Having come to sell arms in the early 1700s they took advantage of what seemed like endless conflict on the continent, whether it be new arrivals fighting the natives, the French fighting the British, or the American colonists fighting for independence from the British. It is safe to say, in the 18th century they weren't short of customers. Due to the events in France with fellas like Robespierre kicking up a fuss, their vineyard in France was seized and given to another family, so they made North America their home - just south of the Canadian border in Michigan as it happened.

They are probably the most hospitable family and most generous people I have ever met. They're not exactly

French Canadian but their history is similar to many Frenchies who came to North America. The joint eldest son, Dylan, told me that the vineyard still exists. If I were one of those original Bousquettes I would be fairly annoyed at losing such a beautiful home, however they have found opportunity where most would see despair. The other brother Luc, is named with the French spelling leading me to believe that they are still proud of their French heritage. They are a lovely family and their story of inspiration and perspiration brings the wider story of French-Canadians to life. People coming to North America for the opportunity, some staying in what is modern day Quebec while others moving west or south to other areas.

The French Revolution had shaken Europe. In 1793, Britain and France found themselves at war again. For those in Canada the war was distant, and no battles would be fought on Canadian soil. Even so, the French-Canadians in Quebec would have a tough go of it. The British feared French spies were sneaking into Quebec to stir up revolution while in Paris, people were calling for lands lost in the Seven Years war to be regained. The French delegate to the United States called for a free Quebec, and at one point a French fleet headed for Quebec, but the harsh Canadian winter scared them off.

This rhetoric and threat of Quebec revolting and returning to the French did not help the Quebec population. Throughout Quebec, there were manhunts for alleged French spies and sympathisers. Just being foreign in Quebec made you half guilty. Among the English, there was chatter about trying to remove the French-speaking population. They went after French speaking newspapers and schools as a way of trying to reduce potential opposition. This aggressive rule of the British began to make the French-Canadians feel oppressed, and their differences and alienation from society grew. For those in Quebec, the benefits of being in the Empire were now less compelling. The economic advantages started to get outweighed by the issues of rights and independence. The French-Canadians had their own identity - divided by language and geography from the rest of those in Canada. However, despite this, there were no revolts and no violence, and yet if seemed French-Canadian people self determination would not be tolerated by the British.

Napoleon was kicking up a fuss in Europe and war raged across the continent. In North America, the US had agreed a trade deal with France in which they cut trade ties with Britain. At the same time, the US had recently bought lots of land off France, yet there were gaps in the territories, such as land around the Great Lakes, which border Canada. The British funded natives to fight the Americans. Consequently, the US declared war on Britain – feeling that they couldn't allow Britain to interfere with their internal expansion. They invaded Canada but the attack was halted by the British with native support. There were various battles, with both sides dealing hefty blows to one another. While this war waged in North America, by 1814, fighting in Europe stopped. Hence Britain could fully commit to the war against the US. British troops flooded across the Atlantic and famously burnt down the White House. The fighting continued but gradually both sides lost the will to fight and so a peace deal was signed.

For the French-Canadians, this war was an opportunity for independence. Quebec feared invasion from the US, but it was unclear whether that invasion would bring liberty or simply swap rulers. Meanwhile, Britain was starting to see the importance of Quebec and Canada. They had to defend it – they needed timber for their navy. Hundreds of Quebecois took advantage of this employment, loading ships with timber to be sent to Britain. These men become iconic legends in the history of the French-Canadian people and changed the focus of the post war expectations – from revolution and independence to economic opportunity. More companies now came to Canada to invest and the rumbles of revolution quietened. Quebec was seeing the gains from being part of the Empire. They still viewed themselves as independent people but they were okay with the British Empire as it was bringing economic prosperity. Slowly however, over the next 20 years, the perception changed again and tension grew, across all Canadians but especially within the French-Canadian population.

The Rebellions of 1837 & 1838

Contrary to popular belief, Canada was not always the Empires best-behaved colony. In 1837 and 1838, across the Canadian colonies, the ideas of democracy and liberty ran rampant. Canada at the time still didn't exist as we know it today, it was multiple different colonies. Across both Upper and Lower Canada (two separate British colonies at the time), rebellions, protests and riots sprung up. The bells of democracy that once rung in the 13 US colonies now rung across the Canadian colonies.

The Canadian colonies were still run as a business, as far as the Empire was concerned. Quebec is situated in Lower Canada, which was overseen by the Chateau Clique. This was comprised exclusively of Englishmen, who demanded the French-Canadians give up their French heritage and become anglified. For the Quebecois, this created an intolerable situation. In many ways they were now considered foreigners living in English Canada. Obviously, the majority of the French population were not too happy about this arrangement. Abandoned by France and now being oppressed by Britain - it wasn't exactly what the original settlers had in mind. So the Quebecois took a stand. A certain Louis-Joseph Papineau became the leader, heading a group known as the Patriots. Anger towards the British intensified in Quebec after 1832 when protesters in Montreal were gunned down by British soldiers. Following this incident, Papineau sent a list of demands to the British demanding reform. However, the old, stale, male and pale British aristocracy took the view all was fine. So over the next 5 years, tensions grew and culminated in a revolution in November 1837. It was sparked by the government trying to arrest Papineau. He managed to flee to the US, and in his absence the Quebecois took to the streets in protest.

The British couldn't keep this protest under control like they did in 1832. The revolution spread like wildfire among the French-Canadian population, widening out across Lower Canada. However, the British brought in more troops and ruthlessly put down the revolutionaries, who were not trained soldiers but rather poor working men. The revolution was crushed.

The Battle of Saint-Eustache, where the Government put down an uprising in 1837. 70 of those rebelling died. Lower Canada, Painted 1840 by Lord Charles Beauclerk.

When all seemed lost, the Americans took an interest. Having fought for freedom themselves, they understood the Canadian struggle. They supported Papineau in his attempts to form a republic and sent groups of armed men to help. These American men became known as the Hunter Brothers. Unsurprisingly, the British killed them too. Back in the US government, they realised that a war with Britain was not in the best interest of the US, so they pulled back many of the citizens who were going to help. By the end of 1838, the revolution was dead, but the ideas of freedom and independence among the Quebecois had been born. These ideas live on in the dreams of many French-Canadians up until today.

Britain however, would not make the same mistakes

again and they would not ignore the Canadian demands completely. They sent over a chap called Lord Durham to decide what reforms would be needed. One idea was to unite Upper and Lower Canada, which was abhorrent for Quebecois as it meant they were bundled in with even more Englishmen. This was, however, the start of Canadian unification. For the French-Canadians, their hopes of any sort of self-determination were gone as the British tried to make them a smaller minority within a bigger region. In effect, they were talking about de-frenchifying Quebec, and they sent many of those who had been revolting to Australia, the penal colony of the British Empire.

Moving through the 19th Century

The next half of the century saw much social and political change in Canada. Vast numbers of immigrants poured in – some estimates put it at some 800,000 people. They came for land and timber. From 1815 to 1850 men and women arrived from the British Isles in what became known as the 'Great Migration'. With this immigration, demographics changed, but the French-Canadian population boomed as well, partly due to the strongly Catholic nature of the population.

Politically at this time, governments tended to be short-lived due to a bizarre system. For instance one government only lasted 4 days. The continual uncertainty and chaotic nature of politics made many leaders call for a confederation. The idea of unifying the colonies, with each province retaining some autonomy over its own affairs, was attractive for the French-Canadian people. Being Canadian and also a Quebecois would become a reality. While many felt Quebec should have never joined this federation, let's not forget, it wasn't really up to them, they did belong to Britain after all. Meanwhile, some in London disliked the French-Canadians and wanted them punished for not really integrating into the Empire. Tensions between French-Canadians and English Canadians was evident and especially in

Quebec. For instance Lower Canada voted against reforming the militia to form a Canadian army on the basis that a single army implied that they were one people. The Frenchies couldn't allow that even though the English Canadians were unanimously in support. The divergent nature of Quebec in politics is rooted in the fact that they hold themselves as their own people. The bill reforming the militias was finally passed, not least as the American Civil War was now raging to the south, and the Canadians wanted to make sure they were ready for the worst.

In 1867, Canada was formed as a single nation, with the provinces of Quebec, Ontario, Nova Scotia and New Brunswick. It became known as the Dominion of Canada, with a constitution and all. Even though it was a nation, its foreign policy was under British control. This was also when Quebec became formally known as Quebec. The French-Canadians took two real views on this. George-Etienne Cartiers, a politician, felt they did not need to look on English Canadians as their enemy but rather people to imitate and join. Obviously, there was opposition to this, and many in Quebec felt themselves French-Canadian and under no circumstances would they become entangled with the British. In the formal political union, many also feared what would happen to the French language as, at that point in time, 75% of the Quebec population spoke French. So they established their own legislative assembly in which they governed alongside the House of Commons which was nationwide. Many Quebecers also feared for the future of Catholicism. As a result, many French-Canadians fled to the United States.

During the second half of the 19th century, Quebec desire for independence slowly grew, fuelled by the influential Catholic church, which also ran many schools and hospitals. This desire was founded on religious, cultural, social and political divides and was further strengthened by the execution of Louis Riel in the North-West rebellion. He had been leading the native Cree people in a fight for independence and rights against Canada. Many French-Canadians drew a direct parallel. The sense of oppression grew in line with attempts to make them speak English rather than French and with the increasingly centralised system that was developing through the latter stages of the century. Over the next century, the French-Canadian people would assimilate into Canada, and the scale of the divide would lessen, but the will for independence would not go away.

Moving into the 20th Century

In the year 1896, the first French-Canadian Prime Minister was elected. Wilfrid Laurier was the man and he completely changed the French-Canadian community and Quebec. Laurier fought the influence and power of the Catholic church; he silenced the French-Canadian opposition to Canadian involvement in the Second Boer War down in South Africa while openly acknowledging that "French Canadians are a conquered race". He was as French as French-Canadians can get, being a ninth-generation French-Canadian and born in Quebec. Following the death of his mother, he moved to New Glasgow where he familiarised himself with the British.

Learning the English culture but also not forgetting his own, he led the Dominion of Canada until 1911. For the first time it seemed Canada had a leader both the French-Canadians and English-Canadians could support. He oversaw a new wave of immigration that came to Canada in the early years of the 20th Century. He utilised that immigration to incentivise many to settle in western Canada. He unified Canada both politically and geographically, building new roads and railways to facilitate travel. Under his leadership, Canada grew tremendously, with the provinces of Alberta and

Saskatchewan being created. Canada, as we know it today, took shape under Laurier. His stature in Canada and his significance to the people is evident - you only have to look at the $5 bill. He transformed politics, bringing French-Canadian voters into a position of power. With him came the realisation that to win elections you need the French-Canadian vote. For many, Laurier was the bridge between two divided people. But let's not get ahead of ourselves, there were still clear cut social divides between the English and the French and, at the end of Laurier's tenure, World War 1 widened these divides again.

Sir Wilfred Laurier, taken in 1906

When war kicked off in Europe in August 1914, Canada was dragged in, being a dominion of the British Empire. At this time, Canada had a population of just under 8 million people, and all those of British descent were committed to helping the motherland. Indeed, many had recently moved from the British Isles. Hence, they were eager to fight even though, at the start of the war, Canada's formal army was the size of a large school. Amazingly, with energy and enthusiasm, Canada grew its army to around half a million men. What is more impressive, to my eyes, is not the numbers they were able to muster, but the quality of the soldiers they were able to produce. Across the war, Canadian troops were regarded as some of the best out there. The first 30,000 Canadian soldiers set sail on 3rd October 1914.

Canada's first real involvement in the war was on the Western Front at Ypres in 1915. The battle of Ypres was one of the most costly in history. As the battle kicked off, the Germans rained poisonous gas on the Allied trenches. The gas sunk into the British and French lines, and men began to choke and drown in the poisonous fumes. Thousands of Allied troops retreated. The Germans had won acres of land without firing a shot.

The allied retreat left vast swathes of land for the Germans to move into. It seemed bleak for the Allies. Until that Canadian force, which had never seen battle before, was thrown in at the deep end. They quickly filled the gaps where men had retreated. The Germans attacked, now pushing to take the trenches but the Canadians held firm. Even in the face of a second gas attack, they did not budge. The Canadian men suffered.

This heroic stand to keep the Germans back came at a heavy price. Thousands died. Their once strong young bodies now limp in the mud of Ypres. Their bravery is incomparable. All this killing occurred at a place called Kitchener's Wood. The Canadian sacrifice on this day is often regarded as one of the defining moments of the war, not just for Canada, but for all nations involved. Throughout the early part of the war, the Canadian troops fought in and around British soldiers, but gradu-ally things changed, and in 1917, the Canadian force was made purely of Canadians. It was symbolic of how, through this war, they were becoming their own people. The Canadian Corps was born. However, there were next to no French-Canadians, and thus the divide between the English and French Canadians grew. All across Canada, people made their feelings towards Quebec clear. Many felt the bravery from these English-Canadian troops was being snubbed by French-Canadians.

My great Grandfather fought in World War I on the

Western Front. Ronald 'Ronnie' Rushton was his name. He fought in the Battle of Loos where the Allies lost some 60,000 men while the Germans lost 26,000. He was shot 2 inches from the heart. My Grandmother (his daughter) said the bullet went in the front and straight out the back. Apparently, he was shot in the perfect place, as it didn't pierce an artery or puncture a lung. My Grandfather, his son in law, spoke to him about it. Ronnie said he saw the German take aim and he assumed that would be it. Luckily for me, he survived. He also lost a toe to trench foot. It was the first time gas attacks had been used in the war and was a major British defeat. Why am I telling you this? Well, it would be the Canadian troops who would reclaim the territory for the Allies. I might add, the Canadians did it with only 12,000 troops. They incurred about 9,000 Canadian casualties (killed or injured) retaking the position, while inflicting 25,000 casualties on the Germans. As for my great Grandfather, Ronnie, he did not serve again, probably understandably.

In 1917 the war was in the balance. One big victory could turn the tide of the whole war. The Canadian Corps would not disappoint. They took Vimy Ridge, which was a hugely important strategic position and indeed, would prove pivotal. The man to lead them in this was no other than Arthur Currie. Currie was inventive with his tactics but had a problem. For the attack to work, the Canadian Corps would need a lot more men. This is where the French-Canadians come in.

For French Canadians, this was not their war and they felt no loyalty to either Britain or France. As we know from history, France had left them, and Britain had oppressed them. Many French-Canadians in Quebec roared in anger when asked to fight in Europe – they felt they should be fighting for the freedom of Quebec. However it is worth noting some Quebecers still held a sense of loyalty to France and although very few in number, some did go to fight on the Western Front to protect France. Tensions were high in Quebec as, at the time, French was being removed from certain schools and the social divides between the two peoples seemed to be nearing a breaking point. For many French-Canadians, this was a time of high animosity to both Britain and the English majority in Canada. When the war started, very few Quebecois signed up in comparison with the other provinces. In 1916, Canada introduced conscription, and (as I am sure you've gathered), they weren't best pleased. Riots broke out in Quebec - 15,000 French-Canadians took to the streets in anger and outrage. The army suppressed the riot. The confrontation between the Quebecers and the army left hundreds wounded, and 4 dead. The war was meant to be in Europe, but it now seemed to be in Quebec. Only 5% of able fighting Quebecers fought in the European war, making a statement unlike any other before that they were not Canadian. Demands for French-Canadian independence would grow throughout the century.

However, the Canadian government treated the Quebecois like any other Canadians, namely, they were expected to contribute to the war effort. Ultimately a French-speaking regiment was formed, despite the feelings of many of those in Quebec. The 22nd Regiment was born and headed for Europe, and the battle of Vimy Ridge would be their finest hour.

Through the war, Canadian soldiers became feared among German camps. They became known for being ruthless, fearless and relentless. What is clear to me is that when the Canadians were at war, they would not stop until they had won or died. Many observers called Canadian soldiers overly aggressive and that they should have taken more prisoners. They reported that Canadians wanted revenge for their compatriots who had died at the hands of Germans. One Canadian soldier in the war called R.C. Germain wrote after the fight for Vimy Ridge -"After losing half of my company there, we rushed them, and they had the nerve to throw up their hands and cry 'Kamerad.' All the 'Kamerad' they got was a foot of cold steel... While I blew out their brains with a revolver". "Kamerad" is German for surrender. I don't think these actions, whether right or wrong, should not be judged by those who did not fight on the battlefield. The First World War was clearly a horrific conflict, with gassing and disease, and I suspect more pain than any civilian could understand. I am wary of judging these people too harshly. I think the Canadian General Walter Natynczyk put it best, "The further you are from the sound of guns, the less you understand".

Indeed, the war was of a scale of unparalleled brutality. For Canada, the war had many battles, but none quite as defining and inspiring as that of the battle for Vimy Ridge. This was Canada's bold defiant attack against the Germans. It showed glimmers of unity among Canadians as French and English Canadians fought side by side. Whilst researching this, I was astounded by the high reputation of the Canadian troops, becoming known for their ruthlessness and tenacity. This was the gritty western front where inches were fought over for weeks and where "No-man's land" loomed between Allies and Germans. So, Vimy Ridge was the moment that Canada would help turn the tide of war. The British artillery battered the Germans for days on end. But the British weren't aiming for the Germans. They were aiming for the no-man's land barbed wire to help reduce the challenges this posed. No-mans land was a lifeless hell all of its own. Trees that once stood tall were now splintered and broken by the explosions of shells. Shells that created craters so large that horses would fall in and not be able to climb out. Fields of mud lay impenetrable as barbed wire and traps loomed for one misplaced step. Battle loomed in the skies too, with the eerie noise of bombs dropping haunting the soldiers on the ground. If you want to get a feel of WW1, watch the film "1917". It was like nothing we could imagine today. Boys leaving their homes, leaving their loved ones, for a misery that almost defies imagination.

In the lead up to the actual battle, the Allies took to the skies on the basis that if you wanted to win the land, first, you had to win the air. Many Allied pilots were killed in tenaciously fought dog fights. As mentioned, British artillery battered all the known German artillery.

6-inch Naval gun on "Percy Scott" carriage, firing over Vimy Ridge behind Canadian lines at night.

Lines and lines of Germans lay ahead. As the artillery rained down, those Canadian soldiers pushed forward to prepare to attack the German positions. The Canadians were inventive - rather than cross the open top of the battlefield, they found hidden sewer systems and tunnels which helped them get closer to the German lines. Indeed, when they emerged, they were only just over 100 metres away from the Germans. Even so, if spotted as they emerged, it would be slaughter. So the Canadians were smart, creating smokescreen with canisters, thus masking their exit from the sewers. The four Canadian divisions were ready; the whistles screamed, and they charged over the top. Their charge was so rapid and hidden, the Germans were stunned, and before they knew it, the Canadians were in their trenches and all around them.

Canadian machine gunners dig themselves in, in shell holes on Vimy Ridge. This shows squads of machine gunners operating from shell-craters in support of the infantry on the plateau above the ridge. 1917.

However, German lines behind the front lines taken by the Canadians opened their machine guns on the Canadian soldiers. The Canadians continued to charge, men falling to the left and right, but fearing defeat more than death. The Canadians overwhelmed the secondary lines with their speed and fearlessness. They were so quick, German reinforcements did not get there in time despite being relatively close. After only three days, the entire Ridge belonged to those brave Canadian soldiers. The Germans were stunned, and so were the Allies. The Canadians had earned the respect and admiration of the British soldiers and indeed all the soldiers in the war. They defeated the Germans at Vimy Ridge, and with it, the Allies were slowly able to turn the tide of the war. However, the casualties were heavy, and not just from the fighting. In the nights after the battle, many had to sleep outside, and the cold and wet meant that many passed away in their sleep.

Canadian stretcher bearers carrying a wounded soldier through the mud of the Ypres Salient, 1917

One of the Canadian soldiers who demonstrated fear-lessness that day was Thain Macdowell. Following the Canadian artillery barrage, Macdowell went ahead of the divisions to check the damage caused before the main offensive. He went with two other men, Kobus and Hay, and they quickly came under machine gun fire from two German machine gun nests. Pinned down and under fire, they sheltered behind a small hillock of mud. He had two grenades in his pocket. So, this Quebec born renegade lobbed them into each machine gun nest. After the explosions, he peeked over the small mound of mud to see one nest blown to pieces with the machine gun operators dead. The other machine gun post was damaged, but one man was still alive. Macdowell rose from his mound, made direct eye contact with the machine gunner, and marched towards him. In fear, seeing this relentless, fearless, mud splattered man striding towards him, the German turned and ran. Macdowell raced after him. Behind the German first line, the gunner slipped into a tunnel. Macdowell saw this but returned to reunite with his two fellow soldiers before following.

At the edge of the tunnel, Macdowell shouted for the man to surrender and that no harm would come to him. Silence. He shouted again, but still, no response. Macdowell carefully and cautiously headed into the tunnel. 5 metres in, there was a ladder which dropped down into another hole, and only a small flickering light at the end. Macdowell was not going to let the German machine gunner get away. Moments like these decide battles. If he did get away, he could call for reinforcements so Macdowell knew he would have to plunge into the deep dark hole. He told his two colleagues to wait outside and descended into the unknown. Bravery does not even begin to describe it. The climb down was long and daunting (it was actually 75 feet deep, although of course he did not know that at the time – each foot probably felt like a marathon). Gradually he progressed into the darkness. It was quiet and almost completely dark.

After a while, he went round a corner. 77 German rifles

were now pointed at him. He was face to face with 2 officers and 75 soldiers, including the gunner he had been chasing. It looked as though he had found where the German soldiers hid during the Canadian artillery barrage. Knowing that he had to do something or be taken captive, he quickly shouted for the other Canadians to attack (making the Germans think there was a much larger Canadian force above). Just like that, the Germans laid down their weapons. They all surrendered, thinking the Canadians had taken the land above during the artillery barrage. But what to do now? The Germans would soon find out Macdowell was lying – he had no army, just two mates up at the top. So he improvised and sent the Germans up in groups of twelve without their rifles.

So, up they went up in their twelves, up the narrow passageway, to come out to see Kobus and Hay, and no one else. Embarrassed and humiliated, one soldier tried to grab a rifle and shoot Kobus and Hay. They were faster, and shot him dead. This was a clear warning to the Germans not to try anything. So Kobus and Hay tied up the groups of Germans in turn as they surfaced. They then held this position for four days and nights. Under heavy shell fire, they kept their little camp. Artillery battered them, but they did not budge, although Macdowell was injured in the hand from one shell fragment. Finally, the Canadian divisions caught up with them during their advance on the ridge.

Macdowell was awarded the Victoria Cross for his bravery. Following this, he said: "We had a great time taking them prisoner".

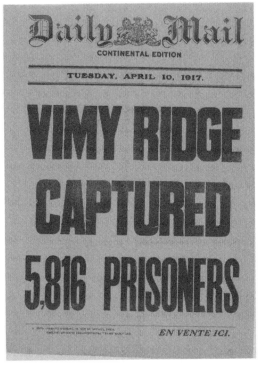

Front page, Daily Mail, Tuesday, April 10, 1917,
reporting the number of German prisoners captured
at Vimy Ridge

I think we all know who helped write that headline...

Thain Macdowell taken in 1919

Macdowell, although not French-Canadian, was from Quebec and illustrated that, although Canadians may have a reputation for being polite and friendly, when in combat, they are fearless. It also highlights the bravery and full commitment by English Canadians, in stark contrast to most of the French-Canadians. Back in Quebec, the riots continued and many English-Canadians felt betrayed. The rift between the two peoples was growing…

Following the war, Spanish flu hit Quebec hard with 14,000 deaths. However, the 1920s saw Quebec go from a rural to an urban focus. People were buying cars, and the economy in Quebec began to boom. Before people realised, Quebec was the second wealthiest province in Canada. Despite this economic prosperity, they did not have self-governance and the calls grew stronger for them to decide their own economic policy to target this growth. Nationalists took up the idea, and the Quebec independence movement was born. It would remain in its infancy for several decades still. However, the economic prosperity did not last - post-war Britain and its Empire fell into recession. The unemployment rate grew rapidly so when the Great Depression hit in 1929, Quebec was hit hard.

The economic growth in the mid 1920's led many Quebecers to invest in the stock market. So when it crashed, they felt it personally. The government tried various new schemes to provide jobs to tackle the unemployment rate that had reached 30%. The same economic issues in other countries triggered high immigration to Canada, as people tried to escape the challenges at home. Racism and hatred of foreigners grew. Many felt they were taking local men's jobs. The reality is everyone felt it. Quebec has always had an animosity to outsiders, and had long fought to keep their culture and people safe and uncorrupted. The combination of immigration and economic hardship saw reactionary views boom in Quebec.

Quebec City in 1920

In 1935, the first real calls for complete Quebec independence rang out. The movement was popular among the young and generally orchestrated by an organisation known as 'Young Canada'. Lionel Groulx was the figurehead for the movement, and much of the youth viewed him as the man to deliver Quebec independence. Groulx took their cause to the Congress of French Language and called for the creation of a French speaking state. The newly-elected premier (head of Quebec), Maurice Duplessis denounced this idea. Many Quebec nationalists did not want total independence but rather high levels of autonomy while remaining part of Canada. The move to independence faltered as consensus was lost. But it was evident that Quebec nationalism was on the rise, even if some did not see it as beneficial. The movement had begun and, for the more extreme, independence was the only way forward. Duplessis, however, stuck to a traditionalist and hardline "Quebec first" policy, strengthening the church, arguing with intellectuals, and maintaining French-Canadian culture. Abortion and divorce were made illegal and the rift with the rest of Canada became clearer.

Maurice Duplessis in 1936

Another movement was also growing in Quebec - communism was on the rise. Duplessis, however, was quick to suppress this, authorising police to padlock the doors of houses and buildings in which communists lived and gathered. Fascism was also on the rise. The Christian National Socialist Party actively supported Hitler. Their anti-Semitic policies actually gained some support from conservatives. However, when war was declared in 1939, the party was banned. The real event between the two World Wars was the birth of a formal political movement for Quebec independence.

World War II

"War makes rattling good history but peace is poor reading" - Thomas Hardy

When World War II broke out after Britain and France declared war on Germany, Canada was pulled in. They did not jump in from the get-go, rather they waited over a week to declare war. They did not want to be another Commonwealth nation blindly following Britain. It is thought 10% of Canada's population ended up fighting in the war. The government was eager not to let the war create more problems with Quebec. However, this failed drastically. Duplessis wanted to borrow money to create jobs and fund them through the war. However, he had managed Quebec's finances poorly, and now they were in some trouble. He even went to New York asking for money. Knowing that raising taxes for his inability to manage the economy would be political suicide, he called a snap election and blamed the economic problems on the outbreak of war. He asserted that Quebec would not participate in the war, but his overall mismanagement of the Quebec economy, coupled with his failure to accept any responsibility led to Quebec becoming politically chaotic and volatile. Nationalists grew in numbers while the Canadian government intervened more as they saw this election as key to avoid Canada breaking apart. The problems were similar to those that played out in WWI

– with economic issues coupled with a population who felt neither French nor English, so why should they fight for them? Conscription again became a huge issue.

But then, the landscape changed. The English opposition in Quebec who ran against Duplessis won the election. The liberals who had beaten him had vast financial backing from the rest of the country. Many Quebecers deserted Duplessis as they felt he was using the war as an excuse for his mismanagement of the economy. Canada (and Quebec) would play a pivotal part in WWII, specifically they helped keep Britain alive following the collapse of France. Canada was Britain's closest member of the Commonwealth (both in distance and economically). Quebecois and French-Canadians joined up wholeheartedly. It seemed the divides of the past were healing, for now anyways.

Britain was in dire straits in 1941 and 1942, and Canada was too small to make any significant impact in getting them out of the hole. However, by 1942 Canadian troops were in Britain waiting for battle and many other natural resources went straight to Britain to help them build and prepare for battle. So Canada had a duel impact – both off the battlefield and on it. Indeed, some of the French-Canadian soldiers became legendary for their bravery. Canada's navy helped guard Allied ships across the Atlantic and resisted the Japanese in the Pacific. However, Canada's main impact was the European land war, which is where many French Canadians went.

The Battle of Ortona, during the invasion of Italy, was a tough battle. The Adriatic seaside town became the front for Canadian advances into fascist Italy and saw conflict and conquest reminiscent of its Roman Empire days. The Allies invaded Italy to topple Germany's ally and to divert German and Italian troops so that, when the D-day landings came, they had one eye on Italy. Each building became a battle in itself. The narrow streets meant that both Germans and Canadians had to enter buildings to flush out snipers and enemy soldiers. Rifles were rendered useless. It was hand to hand, knife to knife. Buildings collapsed from the fire of tanks and explosions of grenades. The Adriatic coast was seeing battles the like of which they had not seen for centuries.

*Canadian soldier firing at a German position at
Ortona*

Canadian soldiers firing a mortar into Ortona

The battle could have ended as a German victory if it weren't for the use of new innovative tactics by the Canadians. The tactics became known as 'Mouse-Holing'. Long story short, the Canadians blew holes in the side of buildings so that Canadian troops could travel through the buildings rather than out in the open streets, where they were easier targets for tanks and snipers. So Canada won the battle and continued their drive in Italy. French-Canadian troops fought alongside English-Canadian troops. Although they had their differences, they had one common goal. Win the war.

Canadian soldiers also played a massive role in the Normandy Landings, also known as D-Day. The goal was to land in occupied France and steamroll through

Europe to liberate the fallen nations. Five beaches were targeted - the US had two, Britain two also and Canada had their own – Juno beach. Here Canada would announce itself as equal to Britain and the US, two countries far greater economically and politically. It was their finest hour in among a horrific loss of human life. It was do or die for the Allies. A loss here would mean continental Europe was lost for good, the Nazi machine would stay undefeated, in all their evil. The Canadian in charge of the assault was Major General Rodney Keller. He led the amphibious assault over the 7-kilo-metre long beach. Juno was one of the most heavily fortified. Many who landed were French-Canadian. The divisive politics that had been stirred up in Quebec in the years prior were forgotten. They stood as one people.

So on 6th June 1944, 14,000 Canadians gathered in their landing craft and headed for Nazi-occupied France. Crammed in like livestock, occasional waves soaking them, they crossed the Channel, with rifles in hand. Many prayed for good luck, and to give thanks for the lives they had led. Then, after hours of forced inactivity, the landing craft crashed into the wet sand of the beach, officers shouted charge and blew whistles and they charged headlong into the defending gunfire.

Machine guns quickly cut down many men. Still, they charged. Mortars pounded the shore and did further damage but still they charged up the beach. Brothers fought along brothers and died along with them too.

Puddles of seawater soon turned red as the German fire continued. Trying to aim their rifles to return the fire, they did the best they could. Men upon men laying down their lives, fighting with valour, they pushed on up the beach until they reached the base of the German defences. They were close now. The loud thud of fire thundered everywhere until, suddenly, a colossal explosion roared from one particular German tower. It had blown apart. The German bunkers were now overrun with Canadian troops. They had secured the beachheads.

The numbers do not really tell the full story, but here they are. Of the 14,000 Canadians who landed, 360 were killed and 574 were wounded that day. French and English Canadians fought side by side. Although different, it was truly a powerful symbol of how the two peoples were both Canadians. They fought, under the Dominion of Canada's flag they were one. The Canadians were the first to push inland, starting to liberate town after town. Within a year, the Nazis surrendered. The bravery of these men stopped the fascist Axis powers, with all its horrors. D-Day is remembered as one of the greatest military achievements of all time. Daring and bold it was a success. But the cost was high, overall 946 Canadians died.

*Canadian troops coming onto Juno beach to reinforce those who
originally landed and took the beachheads.*

These Canadians also played a significant role in liberating the Netherlands and Belgium in the last year of the war, having pushed north from Normandy. There are stories of them giving their own rations to the starving civilian population, along with blankets and other supplies. The Netherlands and Canada are still close today. In freeing the Netherlands and Belgium, many more Canadians died, for example, at the Battle of Scheldt, which was key to establish the supply route via Antwerp. This saw 5 weeks of hard fighting (the Germans had flooded the terrain to slow the Allies) and the Allies lost almost 13,000 men, of whom half were Canadian.

As mentioned above, the French-Canadians dived

headfirst into the war. They hold their history in their hearts proudly, having fought, rebelled and rioted for their identity. WWII brought out the best of them as a people, leaving the Quebec nationalism at home, and focusing on winning the war for Canada. One French-Canadian soldier illustrates this fighting spirit better than most. Léo Major. Remember the name. Having fought in the D-Day landing, he became a battle-hardened soldier. Following D-Day, he became a scout working behind enemy lines, on one occasion stealing a book of German codes. When returning to the Allies line, he stole a German tank. However, as he approached, they shot at him (for obvious reasons!). He quickly climbed on top of the tank to show he was friendly. Afterwards, he thanked them for their poor aim. An Englishman was in charge and asked for the German code book, only to be told that it was captured by a Quebecer and thus it was be handed to a Quebecer. This man was a staunch Quebec patriot.

Another time, Léo was sent ahead of his unit to scout enemy activities ahead of the Allies advance. Much to his surprise, he encountered an SS squad. In the fire fight, he killed four of the SS soldiers but was himself injured. A phosphorus grenade damaged his left eye. He was sent to a field hospital and had to wear an eye patch from that point. They tried to send him home, back to Quebec, but he refused. He would fight one-eyed. He stated, 'I only need one good eye to aim a rifle.' and before long, he was back fighting the Germans, now as a scout and as a sniper.

In 1944 he was involved in the Battle of Scheldt where he was tasked with finding 50 Canadian soldiers who had gone missing whilst on patrol. He headed off, during a rainy night, his eyepatch making it even harder to see enemies. He went alone, hiding from enemies as he went. He failed to find the missing 50 men but he came across a German garrison. As they slept in their deeply dug trenches, he drew his rifle and woke up a loudly snoring Nazi officer. The officer kept quiet as the eye-patched Léo seemed more than ready to kill him. Léo told the officer to tell his men to follow him. As he asked, one German grabbed his rifle, but Léo shot him dead. Three other German soldiers tried the same and met the same fate. He yelled, "Achtung hondenhocht" which means "complete attention" and the scared, wet, tired German troops quickly surrendered. There were over 100 men.

Léo marched these German soldiers back to the Allied lines, travelling at night. Suddenly a crackle of gunfire burst the silence. German troops guarding a local town attacked them, first with guns and then with artillery. They were shooting their own men out of anger and disgust with how they had surrendered. The ability of the SS soldiers to kill their own had a profound effect on Léo. Luckily for him, while in the firefight, an Allied Sherman tank came to his aide. So Léo marched his prisoners back to his camp, where he handed over 93 SS soldiers to his shocked commander. Léo was a maverick, and a one off, but he illustrates the nature of the Quebec population from whence he came. Fight for what you believe and never give up, even if the odds are stacked against you.

Léo continued fighting through the war, and in 1945, he was in the Rhineland. While travelling, his vehicle hit a mine and exploded. Everyone in the vehicle died apart from Léo. In the incident, he had broken both ankles, four ribs and his back in three different places. He was taken to a hospital in Belgium where he slowly healed. The hospital demanded he be sent home but again he refused. He rejoined Allied forces as they pushed through the Netherlands. I'm not sure how a man suffers those injuries and still fights but, in April 1945, the Allies were preparing to take the Dutch town of Zwolle. They had little information on the enemy ahead – their manpower, supplies, and artillery capability. They needed to know so who do you think was asked to scout it out?

Léo and another soldier named Willie Arsenault headed off. The Allies had been keen on bombing the town but Léo and Willie convinced them to wait to try to prevent loss of civilian life. Under cover of darkness, Léo and Willie snuck to the outskirts of the town. They saw some German soldiers on patrol. Suddenly, they opened fire and Willie was shot dead. The rattle of grenades in his bag had given him away. Léo retaliated, shooting two Germans dead, before the others ran away. Léo was fuming. Willie had been his close friend so he took his friend's ammo, grenades and submachine gun and determined to avenge Willie.

He hijacked a nearby German car and took the submachine gun of the soldier who had been driving it. He made the soldier drive him to a bar where he located a French-speaking German officer, confiscating his pistol. Léo told him of the incoming artillery barrage which would kill not only German soldiers but civilians too. Léo hoped the man would evacuate his troops and so, returning his pistol, told him to get his men out of there, and he let them drive off. He had gambled. Either the Germans would return and attack, or they would retreat. Following this, Léo searched the town looking for German soldiers. He was armed with his three submachine guns, and gunned down soldiers as soon as he saw them, in revenge for Willie. He made as much noise as he could - throwing grenades and firing his submachine guns. His idea was to confuse the enemy into thinking he was a much larger force. As he moved through the Dutch streets he continued to kill German soldiers. By moving constantly he gave the impression of there being soldiers all over the place. Gradually he picked up prisoners. Once he had ten, he marched them back to the Allied lines. Again and again, he did this, capturing approximately 100 German soldiers. During the night he had to take a breather every now and then, cuz you know taking an entire fortified town single handedly is hard. He also broke into civilian houses, to rouse support from the locals – who helped once they knew he was Canadian.

Léo wasn't done. He made his way to the Gestapo headquarters where he started a fire. He then tried his luck at the SS headquarters, where he engaged in a firefight, killing four before moving on. While running from street to street, he came across some blokes, who turned out to be members of the Dutch Resistance so Léo told them that the town had been liberated. They got all the local men and women to take to the town hall and reclaim the town. The Germans fled. Léo Major, Quebec born French Canadian had liberated the town of Zwolle single-handedly. By the way Zwolle had a population of 50,000. The story grew and Léo became known as 'the one-eyed ghost' in German camps. In the telling, the reputation of Canadian troops more widely grew as being the bravest and most fearless soldiers.

Following the battle, Léo went back to pick up Willie's body and returned it to the Allied lines. The morning after Léo's heroics, the Allies entered the town without having to fire a single bullet. Léo had saved the entire town from destruction and had saved the civilians from the collateral damage that would have resulted. It seems fitting that a patriotic Quebecer felt so strongly to liberate these Dutch men, women and children from Nazi rule. Quebec too has been the under the rule of others for much of its history. Following the war, Léo went back to Quebec and returned to his old job of pipefitting. So if you're ever in the Netherlands and wonder why they love the Canadians, "the Saviour of Zwolle" Léo Major might have something to do with it.

Oh and one last thing, he never mentioned his wartime exploit. Whilst living back in Quebec, he hadn't told his son of the events that had conspired in The Netherlands. However, one day a group of Dutch men and women from Zwolle flew to Canada to say thank you for all he did. Saving them and their town. As you would imagine, his son was surprised, to say the least. There is one quote from the American General George Patton that makes me think of Léo Major, "The object of war is not to die for your country but to make the other bastard die for his"

Léo Major with his trusty eye-patch

These moments are held dear in the hearts of Canadians, both French and English. By the end of the war, about 20% of the Canadian military was French Canadian. The country had come together in its fight against tyranny and fascism. Where World War I opened wounds, World War II seemed to be healing them. Even in Quebec, the cries for independence were quietened. However, they would re-awaken through the latter half of the century.

Moving into the 1950s

In the years after the war, French and English Canadians really became one people for the first time. A baby boom occurred, and in 1951 a quarter of Quebec was under ten years old. Immigration also increased drastically, with less from Britain and more from other European nations. However, the harmony of the war years ended as Duplessis won the next election. In 1948, he officially made Quebec's flag the fleur-de-lis, which would become the symbol for French Canadian nationalism.

fleur-de-lis

The 1950s saw a clash between English and French speakers over education. It was commonly acknowledged that universities were imperative in protecting both culture and language. The central government had the ability to intervene in universities and education. When they began to subsidise universities, much to the dislike of Quebecers, most Quebec universities refused. It was a clear statement that Quebec was its own society with its own rules. It marked the growth of the rift between English and French. The Quebec born prime minister at the time, Louis Saint-Laurant said that Quebec was just like any other province. However, it wasn't. The divides between French and English were clear, and politicians ignoring these challenges did not help solve them.

The Quiet Revolution 1960's

Quebec was changing, and in the 1960s, it changed drastically, both socially and politically. For the first time, the French-Canadians were starting to really unite. This is known as the Quiet Revolution. There needs to be an emphasis on the Quiet - it was peaceful and was about reform and democratic change rather than riots and blood.

For years Duplessis had defended the church and left social and cultural issues to them. He was hands-off with the economy, and very clearly against any sort of federal involvement in Quebec. However, Duplessis passed away in 1959, and a man named Paul Sauvé took his place as the Premier of Quebec. At the next election, Sauvé stood to continue the legacy of Duplessis while also doing things his own way. He ran with the Union National Party, and in the 100 days he was in office, Quebec had changed. A lot. He brought in much of what Duplessis had been opposed to, specifically changing the role of the church. He was also more hands of with the economy. He made huge reforms, increasing the minimum wage along with worker conditions. Education was also greatly encouraged and strengthened under him. This reform was the start of a period in which Quebec would go from a traditional conservative Catholic province to a more modern and secular society. Quebec politicians rallied behind Sauvé. There was lots of literature published at this time, for instance the 'Impertinence of Brother anonymous' which was read across Quebec. It called for change and looked to the future.

However, the Liberal party won the general election in 1960. Jean Lesage took over. But Sauvé's days in office were significant. As the Premier, Lesage stood for the anti-Duplessis and anti-Union National Party. Over the coming years, Quebec would be transformed under Lesage. Public hospitals were established and electricity was nationalised. A pension plan was created. The Ministry of Education was established, and finally, a welfare plan was put in place. Jean Lesage made people proud to be from Quebec as their province prospered. Quebec became more progressive, and almost all of Quebec saw this as a good thing. It was as though they were finally being brought into the modern world. It also integrated more into Canada when, in 1969, the official languages act formally recognised French as an equal language across Canada.

Along with these Canada wide changes, Quebec had tasted freedom, deciding their own laws and destiny. With this came an increase in nationalism. All across the world nations were declaring independence from old colonial masters. It was clear that many in Quebec felt that their time had come. They protested visits from the Queen. They were adamant - she was not their monarch. Nationalism was on the rise and the President of France came to Quebec and in a speech he called for Quebec independence - 'vive Quebec libre'. He captured the dreams of the thousands, who came onto the streets, stamping on British flags and vandalising Canadian symbols. Violence spiked. In 1963 the Front de libéra-tion du Québec (FLQ) set off bombs in Montreal. The FLQ did not stop there. In 1970 they kidnapped both a British diplomat and a Cabinet member. The Cabinet member, Pierre Laporte, was murdered by the terrorist group. The president of Canada at the time, Trudeau (not the one who rules today but his father), placed Quebec under martial law and invoked the war measures act. This was despised by much of the Quebec population, although most did not approve of the actions by the FLQ either. In Quebec, the ministry of culture was created with the sole purpose of protecting French culture. In addition to this, the Parti Quebecois was founded in 1968, around the idea of nationalism and independence. This trend continued through the Seventies.

The 1980 Referendum

This rise in nationalism soon found its way into formal politics, with Quebec making its feelings towards the rest of Canada known. In 1976 the 'Parti Quebecois' were elected on the mandate that they would provide a referendum on Quebec's sovereignty. It would be under the title of "Sovereignty Association" which basically meant independent but economical tied together. In June 1979 the Premier of Quebec, René Lévesque, announced the referendum. The question put to the people said that Quebec would negotiate a new constitution regarding their position in Canada. However the separatists took a hit, as the Liberals had regained power. The local liberal leader rallied the "no" vote. Lise Payette, a women minister in the cabinet, called for all women to vote "no". With the election of the Liberals, it appeared the public had already decided. The referendum saw a 86% turnout with the "no" side winning 60% to 40%. It appeared as though Quebec nationalism was not as strong as it had seemed. Perhaps more importantly, it seemed that women, long subjugated by the old Catholic Quebec, had made the difference. However, this setback did not stop the Parti Quebecois in their fight for Quebec independence. Over the next 15 years, they continued to rally support. Levesque, following the defeat, accepted the loss but stated: "If I've understood you correctly, you're telling me 'next time'". The movement was far from done.

The 1995 Referendum

In the 1980's Canada had ratified new constitutional amendments, which were symbolic of the nation becoming further integrated. All nine provinces signed the new constitutional amendments apart from Quebec. Across the country, Quebec's position in Canada became the sole political debate. Some Canadians felt they just needed to appease Quebec and let them succeed. Towards the late '80s and early '90s, the Ottawa government tried, and failed, to enable Quebec to get to a position where it felt comfortable with Canada. It was clear that the direction Quebec was headed now had far more conviction and tenacity in comparison to the movements of 1980s.

Quebec nationalism was soaring. The 1990s saw almost all French-Canadian Quebecers torn between independence and confederation. The rejection of the new constitutional amendments gave way to a rise in Quebec sentimentalism. Robert Bourassa, the Quebec Premier at the time, vowed to make Quebec independent. None of this "partial sovereignty" stuff. Fully independent. A New Nation. So a referendum was set for 1995. Would this be the year that Quebec and the French-Canadian people finally broke away from the English? The campaign was full of twists and turns. The

Bloc Quebecois, which was the political party heading the Leave campaign, was led by Lucien Bouchard. In the middle of the campaign, he caught a flesh-eating disease and lost his leg! But nevertheless, he still showed up to rallies on crutches. The French President said that he would recognise Quebec if it declared its independence. Meanwhile, Bill Clinton was talking to officials about economic trade deals with Quebec.

Rallies popped up everywhere. Quebec and Canadian flags covered the streets. The nation was gripped. It would be a defining moment. To stick or twist. One rally in Montreal had over 100,000 people all supporting the Remain side. However, unlike 1980, the Leave side had passion and rallies themselves. The Quebec Premier at the time of the referendum, Jacques Parizeau became one of the figureheads of the movement. It appeared being French Canadian in Canada was now becoming more of a political statement than a cultural difference. It didn't stop there. With Quebec possibly leaving, Saskatchewan started talking about leaving Canada and joining the United States. Bizarre, out of nowhere. The point was that Canada's politics were being turned upside down, and the future of the entire nation was in the balance. The extent to which Quebecers identified themselves as independent of English-Canadians depended hugely on the individual. So to swing the referendum for a Leave victory, the Leave side needed to truly galvanise the idea of them being two separate people rather than one.

So we're back to where this story began. The bars were packed, living rooms were full, and Quebecois rallies overflowing. The night of 30th October 1995 arrived. Ever since the Plains of Abraham battle where Wolfe beat Montcalm, the people of Quebec had been under British rule. Every nation and people has turning points in its history. For Canada and the French-Canadians, this was it. Had the merging of the two peoples over recent decades made the Canadian identity stronger than the Quebec identity? The votes were in, and flags waved for both Canada and Quebec. It was close. I mean really close. 93.52% of Quebec came out to vote. The Remain side won. But only by the barest of margins. The No/Remain side got 50.58% of the vote against the Leave vote of 49.42%.

What strikes me is that the English only speakers and allophones (those who speak both French and English) - who by now made up a sizeable chunk of the Quebec population - voted 95% to Remain. The indigenous people of Quebec voted 90% to Leave. 60% of French-Canadians voted to Leave. So one begins to ask, was it really down to the French-Canadian people? But nevertheless, they had lost their shot at independence. Parizeau, the Premier of Quebec, stated in his concession speech that the Leave campaign lost because of "money and the ethnic vote". From then on Quebec nationalism was tainted with ideas of racism. Many Quebecers struggled with the defeat and felt cheated. They felt their people had voted to leave, but non

French speakers and indigenous peoples had thwarted them. Tensions were high. So high in fact that one man broke into the Prime Minister's house with a knife but luckily the Prime Minister's wife stopped him. This moment in Canadian history was truly defining for the French-Canadian and Quebecois people.

French-Canadians and Quebecers are no longer calling for another referendum with the Bloc Quebecois not being the political force it once was. But as we have seen over their history, their nationalism comes and goes in waves. However, as much as they are their own people, increasingly it seems that being Canadian is more important than being a Quebecer or French-Canadian. Their identity today, and the extent to which each person believes in Quebec's independence, is an entirely individual thing. Where the Maori and Afrikaners are divided from their fellow countrymen by race; in Canada, it is solely culture, politics and history that divides them.

Today 12% of Canada cannot speak English. Along with 60% in Quebec who only speak French, the fact that these French only speaking people have not found their independence astounds me. But at the same time, it is a real testament to Canada and its ability to unite people with diverse cultures and histories. I have no doubt we will see another rise in Quebec nationalism, but in many ways, it seems the days of full independence are in the past.

Conclusion

So, there we have it. The End. The main lesson I have taken away from writing this book is just how amazing the past is. Stories that show both the development of an entire people interweaved with those of individuals. It is also clear to me that historical events are determined by individual actions. From the wartime heroics of Léo Major to the more contemporary political courage of de Klerk, I am humbled and impressed by the disproportionate impact individuals can make.

The Land Inherited by the Afrikaners, Maori and French-Canadians is one which they share with others. While their past is proudly remembered and held dear, they will face the opportunities and problems of the future with the courage shown in their past. I wish them all the best as they find their place among other ethnic groups.

———

This Land I Inherited
Hierdie land het ek geerf
Ko tenei whenua i kainga ai e ahau
Cette terre dont j'ai hérité

Sebastian Wright

<u>*About Mr Pedley*</u>

I could not have asked for more from a teacher, through history he taught me more than the battles of the Zulus. He taught me decency and independence. He always describes himself as a maverick and that truly is the best word to describe him. But not a maverick who is unreasonable or selfish, but one who wants to inspire and show students a different perspective. Inspirational both in and out of the classroom.

Mr Pedley also taught me how to enjoy life. He taught at the same school for 40 years. After 5 years I am pleased to be moving on. He told me one history lesson that "I have been many things here, but never bored." Every lesson, cricket match and meal was exciting when he was there.

There has been much said about Mr Pedley, but I will tell you, having sat in the classroom as he taught, that he is kind, compassionate and fundamentally inspiring. I hope one day I can inspire those around me like him.

Mr Pedley and I are still close today, and I am sure we will be for long time still.

About Grampy

Grampy brings history to life. Having served for the British army in Malaya, he tells stories and moments of the past in such detail, explaining things a history book couldn't tell you.

Having grown up in the war right by an U.S. airfield built to help the RAF in their fight against Hitler he used to see the planes take off and fly overhead. He distinctly remembers the American servicemen, telling me that they would always ask "Got any gum chum?" Grampy has taught me that when looking to the past, often it is the mundane and the small things that we remember.

When looking back, I have treasured the moments with my Grandfather. He has inspired me both in writing this book but also in trying to be a good person. I have never met someone as kind and positive. I have not heard him say something nasty about anyone, unless it's a dodgy referee, in which case he's all over them.

As I get older I hope to emulate my Grandfather in his selfless and kind nature. Hopefully, in this book I have brought history to life just like he does.

About the Author

Seb Wright is 18 years old and lives in London. He spent 3 years in New York which engendered a curiosity for other cultures and societies. At home, via his Grandfather, and at school via a particularly inspirational History teacher, he has been lucky enough to be able to nurture this interest. Covid-19, for all its many challenges, has given him the time to indulge this passion. He is going to Leiden University in The Netherlands to study International Relations and Organisations

Acknowledgments

I have tried to give credit to the ownership of the photos used. I have intended to recognise copyright. I am more than happy to correct any omissions or mistakes in future copies. Also, I have only used photos in the public domain. Therefore, I have not been purchasing any of the photos.

The Afrikaners - South Africa

1. A depiction of the Great Trek, The Voortrekkers, No later than 1909, Taken from page 290 of Colvin, Ian (1909). *South Africa*. London: The Caxton Publishing Company. OCLC 893096. painted by J.R. Skelton. Public Domain

2. Depiction of a Zulu attack on a Boer camp in February 1838. date between 1838 and 1882. *Suid-Afrikaanse Geskiedenis in Beeld* (1989) by Anthony Preston. Bion Books: Printed in South Africa. Charles Davidson Bell (1813 - 1882). The painter was Thomas Baines (November 1820 – 1875). Public Domain

3. "The last stand at Isandlwana", 1885, by Charles Edwin Fripp, National Army Museum (SA). Public Domain

4. "The Defence of Rorke's Drift", 1880, painted by Alphonse de Neuville, Art Gallery of New South Wales. Public Domain

5. Photo of Paul Kruger as an Old Man, 1900, P.C.-Archiv, Hamburg. Public Domain

6. Boer guerillas during the Second Boer War, circa 1900, Unknown author. Public Domain.

7. Boers in a trench at Mafeking, 1899, Skeoch Cumming W, Imperial War

Museum. Public Domain.

8. South African forces using a 4.7 inch QF Naval gun in the desert, between 1914 and 1915, "The Times History of the War" Volume VII, published 1916. South African Government. Public Domain.

9. South African officers pose with a captured German flag in Windhoek, 1915, Union Defence Force (poss. Corps of Engineers), Unknown author. Public Domain.

10. An abandoned German Trench in Delville Wood, 1916, Imperial War Museum, John Warwick Brooke. Public Domain

11. Rosamund Everard-Steenkamp. Exhibitor on SASA-related exhibitions c.1898 - 1950: 1931: 1st annual Exh. of Contemp. National Art, SAAG fSANG) with SASA, 7 Dec. - 31 Mar. 1932.

12. Sailor Malan climbing into a Supermarine Spitfire, between 1943 and 1945, Imperial War Museum, Royal Air Force official photographer, Air Ministry Second World War Official Collection. Public Domain.

13. Frederik de Klerk and Nelson Mandela shake hands at the Annual Meeting of the World Economic Forum held in Davos in January 1992. Copyright World Economic Forum (www.weforum.org)

The Maori - New Zealand

1. 'Hunting Moa birds from *Extinct Monsters: A popular account of some of the larger forms of ancient animal life* 1892.' Extinct Monsters by Rev. H. N. Hutchinson, illustrations by Joseph Smit (1836-1929) and others. 4th ed., 1896. Plate XXIII between pages 232 and 233.

2. Murderers' Bay, Isack Gilsemans, 1646, nl:Nationaal Archief, Public Domain.

3. A sketch of Hongi Hika by Major-General G. Robley in 1820, http://www.nzetc.org/etexts/SmiMaor/SmiMaorP001a.jpg. Public Domain.

4. *'The Death of Von Tempsky at Te Ngutu o Te Manu,'* a portrayal of an incident in the New Zealand wars on 7 September 1868. Painted by Kennett Watkins. 1893, Apparently published in the New Zealand Mail.

5. A Maori village, Taken sometime between 1860 and 1889, Photothèque du Musée de l'Homme via French National Library URL, Public Domain.

6. A Maori carving in a New Zealand Trench at Gallipoli, June 1915, Collection Database of the Australian War Memorial under the ID Number: C01157. Public Domain.

7. The War-Dog of New Zealand, 1914-15, Private Owner, Christchurch City Libraries, CCL-PCOLL-91-06a.

8. Members of the World War I Maori Pioneer Battalion taking a break from trench improvement work near Gommecourt, France. Photograph taken by Henry Armytage Sanders on the 25th of July, 1918. National Library NZ on The Commons. Public Domain.

9. The Bulford Kiwi, circa 1919, postcard, Unknown Author. Creative Commons Attribution-Share Alike 3.0 Unported. Public Domain.

10.A Maori soldier after escaping Greece and making it to Alexandria. Taken 1941. George Silk. Denis Clough archive.

11. Members of the Maori Battalion performing the Haka while posted in Egypt, 25 June 1941, Imperial War Museum, National Library of New Zealand. Unidentified New Zealand official photographer; Restoration by Adam Cuerden. Public Domain.

12. A Maori soldier servicing his rifle. May 1943, Tunis, North Africa. Taken by

Laurence Graddock Le Guay. Denis Clough archive.

13. Photo of Moana-Nui-a-Ki wa Ngarimu, taken in 1940, http://beta.natlib.govt. nz/records/22816137. Public Domain.

French-Canadians - Canada

1. Jacques Cartier, painted by Théophile Hamel Circa 1844, Photographed by Wilfredor in Musée national des beaux-arts du Québec. Public Domain.

2. Women coming to Quebec in 1667, before 1927, Library and Archives Canada / Bibliothèque et Archives Canada. Public Domain.

3. 'Death of General Wolfe' by Benjamin West, 1770, National Gallery of Canada/Musée des beaux-arts du Canada. Public Domain.

4. The Battle of Saint-Eustache, Lower Canada, Painted 1840 by Lord Charles Beauclerk. *Library and Archives Canada.* Public Domain.

5. Sir Wilfred Laurier, taken in 1906, William J. Topley, British Library. Public Domain.

6. 6-inch Naval gun on "Percy Scott" carriage, firing over Vimy Ridge behind Canadian lines at night. May 1917, Canada. Dept. of National Defence. Library and Archives Canada. Public Domain.

7. Canadian machine gunners dig themselves in, in shell holes on Vimy Ridge. This shows squads of machine gunners operating from shell-craters in support of the infantry on the plateau above the ridge. 1917. Canada. Dept. of National Defence. Library and Archives Canada. Public Domain.

8. Canadian stretcher bearers carrying a wounded soldier through the mud of the Ypres Salient, 1917. Imperial War Museum. Canadian Official photographer. Public Domain.

9. Front page, Daily Mail, Tuesday, April 10, 1917, reporting the number of German prisoners captured at Vimy Ridge. Library and Archives Canada. Creative Commons Attribution 2.0 Generic. Public Domain.

10. Thain Macdowell taken in 1919, Joseph John Elliott and Clarence Edmund Fry, University of Toronto Archives. Public Domain.

11. Quebec City in 1920, lapresse.ca, Collection Magella Bureau. Public Domain.

12. Maurice Duplessis in 1936, Bibliothèque et Archives nationales du Québec, Studio Dupras et Colas. Public Domain.

13. Canadian soldier firing at a German position at Ortona, 21 December 1943, Library and Archives Canada, Terry F. Rowe. Public Domain.

14. Canadian soldiers firing a mortar into Ortona, 5 January 1944, Lieut. Alexander M. Stirton. Canada. Department of National Defence. Library and Archives Canada, PA-116845. Creative Commons Attribution 2.0 Generic. Public Domain.

15. Canadian troops coming onto Juno beach to reinforce those who originally landed and took the beachheads. Canadian Forces Joint Imagery Centre, Library and Archives Canada. Public Domain.

16. Léo Major, Historisch Centrum Overijssel_Zwolle.

17. Flag of Quebec, Government of Quebec. Public Domain.

Thank you to Julie, Molly and Olivia for all the help in producing the maps and illustrations for this book. Lastly to my Dad for helping edit the book.

Printed in Great Britain
by Amazon